50 WAYS

ADVENTURES IN

TO LOVE

WINE APPRECIATION

WINE MORE

50 WAYS TO LOVE WINE MORE

ADVENTURES IN WINE APPRECIATION

JIM LAUGHREN, CWE

Crosstown Publishing

Chicago

cover design: Amy Cole
interior design: JPL Design Solutions

Library of Congress Catalog Number: 2018900129

ISBN 978-0-9855336-3-2

Crosstown Publishing, LLC
Chicago, Illinois

Printed in the United States of America

**Quantity Discounts Are Available to Your
Company, Educational Institution, or Organization**

For more information contact
sales@crosstownpublishing.com

To Bob,
for all the wonderful
wines and times
we shared.

TABLE OF CONTENTS

INTRODUCTION

L et's talk about wine: wine drinking mostly, but with a nod to wine tasting, winemaking, wine travel, wine buying, wine sharing, wine history, and the varied, innumerable facets of the wine life that comprise wine appreciation. Let's not, however, use our time dissecting dry, boring formulas or sitting through arcane or elitist recitations.

This book is about pleasure. About sharing and camaraderie. About all the best that wine has to offer. Consider, if you will, how satisfying it is to pour some delicious new discovery into a friend's waiting glass. A small act of hospitality, but one that feels so right. There is much to learn, both from and about wine. And, as with most subjects of interest, the more we explore and experience wine, the more we're able to understand and enjoy it. The idea isn't to become oeno-wizards or puffed-up hey-look-at-me wine gurus; our intent is to smile and drink and share and absorb a bit more of what makes wine so appealing.

You may be a long-time lover of wine or newly seduced to its pleasures. One constant for all aficionados, though, is realizing the impossibility of ever mastering this vast subject. Like a great vinous tapestry of detail and distance, of evolution and history, of worship and wild abandon that spans millennia, interwoven throughout the fiber of untold civilizations from a world before technology to one defined by it, wine is beyond any one person's ability to fully absorb or comprehend.

There is always more to learn, another vintage to assess, a new region discovered or re-discovered, another trend or variable or new finding to influence our perception or redirect the focus of our contemplation. And therein lies its beauty: the embrace of it never grows old. Wine is like an inexhaustible font feeding our curiosity, slaking our unending thirst for knowledge and delight.

We could examine the rulers of Mesopotamia, of Sumer and Babylon, the kings of Assyria, leaders of the Hittites and Canaanites, the pharaohs of Egypt, mariners of ancient Phoenicia, citizens and philosophers of Greece and Rome, the grandees of Spain, the dukes of Burgundy, emperors of the Austro-Hungarian empire, the royals of Great Britain, untold admirals and generals, explorers, scientists, artists and patrons, nobles, philosophers, priests and priestesses, statesmen and stateswomen, presidents, premiers, and prime ministers, all of whom savored the wines of their day. But our concern is to enhance *our* experience of wine and how best to love it more! So we need do and learn new things that surprise and delight us, to use mental and physical muscles that we've never applied to wine. We'll smile because we're happy, because we're learning to love, enjoy, and appreciate a wonderful, complex, and delicious gift.

How or when you were introduced to wine is of little consequence. I've known people to enjoy a glass or two of something red or white every night, much as others savor an after-work martini. Same brand, same jug, same regular purchase made with the rest of the groceries, until … one day they break new ground, ask a few questions, and reach for one of the many bottles they've been ignoring. At first just one, then another, then suddenly they are trying everything in sight. After years of routine, of a small but dependable act of comfort and self-indulgence, something builds, a switch is flipped, curiosity rears its delightful head, and their relationship with wine moves to an entirely new level.

I knew a young woman once, barely old enough to drink, with no wine knowledge whatsoever, who wrangled a part-time job in a wine bar and was exposed for the first time to good wine and good wine conversation. Less than two years later she was a sommelier with multiple certifications, working at a busy restaurant and loving every minute of her new life.

A true appreciation of wine is one of those things that presents itself when we are ready to receive it. It requires a perhaps peculiar combination of curiosity and hedonism, with a penchant for enthusiasm and an undercurrent of drive and sustainable focus. An initial flirtation often precedes one's full-blown embrace of wine, of its growing, making, drinking, collecting, sharing, pairing, marketing, of its chemistry, history, societal import, or global expansion. But once bitten....

So, have a little fun, try something fresh and exciting, soak up some new information. Discover just how appealing and engaging the many facets of wine can be. Often the most pleasing, most memorable of wine "moments" occur while we're learning or indulging in something never previously experienced. Hence, this book's objective is to suggest, present, and explore a variety of new or overlooked activities and nuggets of information intended to put a smile on your face and trigger more of those "aha!" moments.

You will notice that I have chosen to capitalize the names of wine grapes, i.e., Chardonnay, as opposed to chardonnay. While this is technically incorrect, it enables you to more easily scan or review chapters or pages for particular wine varieties that may have caught your interest. So I must admit, your enjoyment, dear reader, means more to me than getting another star from the grammar teacher.

I give you now fifty ways to love wine more. Love; like; adore; appreciate. Philosophers and professors of English may object to my use of *love*. So be it; while they're splitting hairs over definitions and the human relationship with inanimate objects, you and I will be swilling some magnificent juice. *Salud!*

1
ONE
ONE

SABER A BOTTLE OF CHAMPAGNE

HORSES REARING, SWORD-WIELDING CAVALRYMEN—black-booted, in gold-braided jackets—waving sabers in victory, hunting their after-battle reward and refreshment. From somewhere a bottle appears and whoosh…with a single sweep of the blade, the top is sliced off. Champagne bursts forth, a fountain of bubbles, as the horsemen pass gushing bottles from one to another and drink deeply in celebration.

Sabering Champagne brings to mind paintings of Napoleon's mounted troops leading yet another charge, vanquishing another imperial enemy. As it should. The art of *sabrage* most certainly originated with the Hussars, Napoleon's famed light cavalry. The drama and energy, the liveliness of those images: mounted troops atop muscular, well-trained horseflesh, hooves flashing and enemies falling, glints of red—crimson flags and ruby scarves, bloodied faces and wild, burning eyes—amid the swirling grays of gunpowder and

"La Charge" © Mark Churms

cannonballs. No wonder the emperor himself is said to have declared, "In victory, you deserve Champagne. In defeat, you need it."

The myth of it, of severing the neck from a bottle of the world's most celebratory wine, resonates somewhere between fantasy and the visceral thrill of victory. How can such a thing be done? How impossible it seems. Surely, you think, there's more to the story, some secret behind the emerald curtain.

And you would be right. Grab a sword; take your best swing at a bottle of bubbly. The likely result ... a mess. Broken glass, a chipped blade, wine spilled and sprayed everywhere. And nary a drop left to drink.

But, as with anything, when you know how it's done, opening that sparkler is not only possible, it's remarkably straightforward and—not to give away all our secrets—a pretty simple endeavor. And hey, it's fun, a rush of adrenaline guaranteed to put a smile on your face. Your audience, whether small or large, just you and your honey or all your friends gathered together, will exclaim, will be dazzled and delighted at your newfound skill. Then they'll want a glass for themselves, of course.

So just how does one go about opening a bottle of Champagne with a sword? And what about all those shards of glass: is it safe to drink that foaming bubbly?

You may have noticed that Champagne bottles are heavier than regular wine bottles. This isn't because they hold more; both

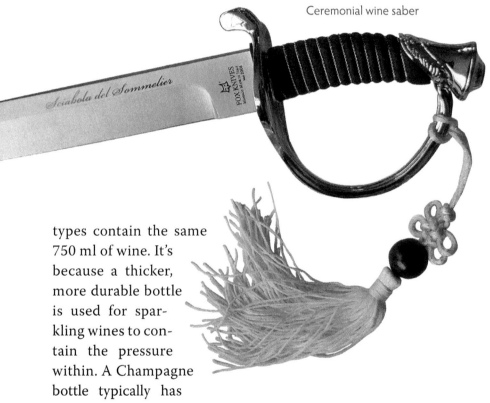

Ceremonial wine saber

types contain the same 750 ml of wine. It's because a thicker, more durable bottle is used for sparkling wines to contain the pressure within. A Champagne bottle typically has seventy-five to ninety pounds per square inch of pressure, close to six atmospheres, almost three times the pressure in your car tires. All that CO_2 that makes your bubbly so bubbly is just waiting for a chance to explode.

In fact, at one time exploding bottles were a real and rather common problem. By the time a shipment of Champagne reached its destination, it wasn't unusual for 25% or 30% of the bottles to be shattered. Glass manufacturers kept making the walls of the bottles thicker and heavier until they eventually solved the problem. What the art of *sabrage* does is take advantage of that pent-up energy.

Because the neck of a bottle is about an inch in diameter while the body of the bottle is somewhere between three and three and a half inches in diameter, there is tremendous force exerted against the reduced area of the narrowed portion. Which in turn means the collar just below the opening is subject to great stress. (Aha, a weak point!) Inspect a Champagne bottle closely and you will see a thin seam running from bottom to top. This creates another point or line of stress. Where the two stress lines meet, where the seam intersects the collar, is the sweet spot, the target, where a bottle's glass strength may be reduced by half.

So now it's clear *where* to impact the bottle with your saber, but do you really need a sword? How about a machete, a bayonet, a hunting knife, or something even less imposing? Yes, yes, yes, and yes. The secret to sabering is using the bottle's internal pressure to blow the top off, not using a sharp blade to slice it off—that's just the illusion, fun and theatrical, the way it looks from outside the curtain.

In fact, it's the back of the blade, known as the spine, and not the edge, that gives the best impact against the target, that point where the underside of the collar meets the seam. Why dull or damage a well-honed blade when all you need is a hard, flat edge with some force behind it? The exception is an unsharpened sword designed specifically for the purpose of sabering.

So, are you ready?

Rather than developing your technique on a pricey bottle of Champagne, it might be advisable to start with a less expensive option, like a Cava, the sparkling wine of Spain, or perhaps an Asti Spumante "Metodo Classico" from Italy. Stay away from Moscato d'Asti or Prosecco, two other popular Italian bubblies as they contain much less pressure. Whatever bottle you choose, there's drama, but there's also a good bottle of wine waiting to be drunk.

A cork popped, blown, or sabered from a bottle of Champagne shoots out at fifty to sixty miles per hour and will travel for thirty feet or more. Best not to point it at your best friend or that Ming vase across the room. Find a place where you can safely shoot a short-range weapon without danger to persons or property. Maybe a back-yard, a driveway, an alley, or a big room devoid of pricey objects.

Next, be sure the bottle is well-chilled. Entirely. Neck and body both. A thirty minute stay in the freezer (watch the time!) should take care of that nicely. And have at hand the implement of discharge. After multiple successes with a custom-designed sabering sword, I am now intrigued by smaller, less obvious tools like butter knives. I have seen a very good sommelier in Seattle do the job, cleanly, with a teaspoon. But to begin, a flat-backed sword, saber, machete, or kitchen knife (a hefty chef's knife or cleaver works fine) makes the ideal tool. Pick it up; handle it; swing it around a few times to get a feel for the heft and weight of your "saber."

To ensure maximum safety, rookies especially are advised to don protective eyewear in defense of flying shards, and to use gloves or a folded towel as an under-bottle cushion in the unlikely event of a bottle shattering—a rare occurrence but it does happen. Also be aware of the implement you're swinging; keep it clear of whatever is best left untouched by sharpened or pointed metal.

The technique—and this is the secret—is to slide the blade, spine side first, up the neck of the bottle along the seam and smack it sharply into the underside of the glass collar. Hit the button right and the top just blows off!

You're not trying to lop the top off, to chop the top off, or even to slice the top off. Your blade should simply be aimed at that magic target, the sweet spot of intersecting stress lines. Much like a golf swing, it's not about force, it's about form and accuracy.

Once you're ready, remove the foil and the wire basket. Six turns will do it, though beware that once the cage is off, the cork is unleashed, so *do not* point the bottle at anyone or anything breakable or vulnerable to the effects of a quickly propelled cork or cork-and-glass bottle top.

Find the seam; turn the bottle so that it's seam side up. Now hold the bottle out, with your thumb in the punt and the body of

it nestled in your palm. With a smooth decisive motion, run your blade up along the seam and smack the collar of the bottle cleanly. Pop! Wow, that's all it takes.

Nice job! Look what you've done. The internal pressure has blown out the cork and the top of the bottle together. Let your bottle foam and blow out any possible

Images: top to bottom

1) Remove the cage (*muselet* in French). It always requires six twists of the wire loop to open. And never point the bottle; it's a loaded weapon.

2) Locate the seam. It's faint but it's there, running along the entire length of the bottle.

3) Glide the blade smoothly along the neck of the bottle, holding your saber at a slight inward-facing angle.

glass shards for a few seconds before holding it upright. Now you can feel free to pour and enjoy the bubbly left in the bottle.

And if you don't succeed at first, try again, slowly and deliberately. This is much simpler than people think. Put on a show. Enjoy yourself. You're looking pretty cool!

In summary, I don't recommend sabering with a sharpened blade. Safety should always be your first concern. Never shake a bottle of sparkling wine or point its uncaged cork at people or pets.

Here's a great online posting by an experienced sommelier: "Not long ago, at an upscale resort in Santa Barbara, CA, I was introducing a guest to sabering. He deftly sliced the top off the bottle …

4) Slide the blade until it impacts the collar. Physics will do the rest.

as planned. The cork and the glass bottle neck sailed across the room and shattered a $3,000 bottle of Cognac ... not as planned! OOOPS!"

Remember, although sabering is much easier than it looks or than most people realize, we're after the thrill of victory, not the agony of a broken collectible. And once the applause has died down—and there will be applause—you are entitled, for all time, to the moniker *sabreur. Santé!*

START OR JOIN A TASTING GROUP

IS ANYTHING MORE GRATIFYING THAN SHARING A NEW, wonderful, or mysterious wine with people whose company you enjoy? Wine drinking has been a communal celebration from the start. It may have been a clan or family group passing the clay bowl around just days after finding and fermenting a batch of wild grapes; or a community offering thanks to its gods of harvest and fertility in the temple of a small Mesopotamian city; or raising cups to the host at ancient Greek symposia; or feasting with the acolytes of Bacchus in preparation for the sacred rites to follow.

Whatever the particulars, indulging in the nectar of the grape has a solid foundation in what we now term social interaction. Together we give thanks; together we celebrate the harvest; together we loosen our tongues, and our passions.

Certainly we have all drunk wine alone. It might have been dinner, at home, yourself and a plate of food quickly prepared, in concert

with a glass of something uninspired. Or on the road, one more meal at a hotel bar and another glass of whatever is being offered by the glass. Wine is good—good wine that is—just about any time in just about any place. But it truly shines, it comes to life, when passed from friend to friend in re-creation of its highest calling.

The good news is that no special skill or background is required to enjoy wine drinking at its most profound level. Get half a dozen friends together, add glasses of wine, and the camaraderie and conversation flow.

A tasting group is simple to assemble and its benefits can be profound. Human interaction gives context and greater meaning to life. Ask the physicians, the psychologists, or the clerics. Establish and maintain vital, interactive relationships and you will probably live a longer, healthier, and more satisfying life. So why not enlist a few bottles of one of humankind's most ancient sacred beverages and a handful of friends (or acquaintances, as the shared experience of wine tasting, toasting, and conversation will convert many of them to life-long compadres) as a down payment on that longer, more satisfying sojourn?

Dare to declare that you have no friends interested in wine or communal quaffing and I'll counter that you've never proposed a relaxed, low-key exploration of that lovely grape product to the more open-minded of your associates. People like to get together—any excuse will do. And positing a wine tasting will almost always elicit yeas from more folks than you expected.

There are many ways to skin this particular cat. One of the easiest is to ask everyone to bring a bottle of wine they enjoy and would like to share. It's fascinating to observe the various responses to each offering, especially when presented blind. People will pronounce which wines they like and which they do not and, when pressed, why. The variety of tastes and the individuality of reactions lead to further discussion and discourse, initially concerning the wine, but with encouragement concerning any- and everything. It's as if a shared chalice opens inner thoughts and feelings.

One approach is to pass the torch of hosting from one member of your group to another. This week you propose the wines and provide the culinary accompaniment; next week, or month, another of your group accepts the pleasure of doing the same, and so on.

If no one is able to provide space, most restaurants would love to offer a room and perhaps a nibble or two at a very reasonable price. And actually, there's something quite simpatico about having friends chip in a few bucks apiece to provide stemware and light appetizers to the group at a local restaurant catering to your concerns.

At one session, you might explore Cabernets from around the world or from a particular time frame, say ten years or older. Maybe your theme is Riojas or white Burgundies from a specific vintage. Or acquainting the group with the wines of a region: trying the wines of

Paso Robles or the Peloponnese. How about a tasting of half a dozen Pinot Grigios or Moscatos if your taste lies in that direction?

The beauty is, there is no wrong or right, no hard and fast rules to a group tasting. It's about sharing the experience and learning a little something along the way concerning the bounty of wine and the abundance of human response. Some groups have members contribute to a common fund that is used to purchase the wines served; other have members supply wines based on that session's parameters.

Some groups are more socially oriented. They may serve dinner and chitchat and exchange news about family and friends and goings on in the world, all while enjoying a selection of wines provided

according to the theme of the gathering. These can be entertaining and enjoyable events, on many levels.

At the other end of the spectrum are the "serious" tastings. Geeks in revelry. No food, no foofaraw, especially as concerns perfume or other aromatic finery. It's all about the wine. A room filled with perfume, no matter how lovely or expensive it may be, precludes the guests from "nosing" the wine and discerning its aromatic profile. Few things are more annoying to a true devotee of the grape than having his or her olfactory sense taken over by an invasion of musk and citronella while attempting to isolate the subtle bouquet of a much-anticipated wine. Over-the-edge aficionados even ban cooking; those sizzling, steak-on-the-grill aromas can be just as disruptive. Any food served at these gatherings is typically prepared either before or after the presentation and appraisal of the wines.

But whatever approach you prefer is the right one for you. Two or three friends dropping by, each bringing a New World Chardonnay, be it from California, Australia, South Africa, Chile or wherever, and then tasting and comparing and deciding which each of you favors is a fun, easy, and informative way to spend an evening and improve your knowledge of a particular variety at the same time.

Or maybe you'd favor a tasting of fifteen Chablis (a decidedly Old World Chardonnay) produced by ten different winemakers, all in the same vintage, each wine to be tasted blind, scored in silence so as not to influence another's assessment, and then discussed in excruciating detail. No food, no flowers, and definitely no eau de toilette. Heaven for the committed grape nut, why-am-I-here confusion for the casual sipper.

As said before, the only guidelines are the ones you want. Many wine lovers belong to more than a single group; one may be social and emphasize the pleasure of each other's company as enhanced by a few glasses of something tasty; another may have greater focus on the wine itself and learning and exploring new aspects of wine and winemaking.

It's all good. Sometimes incredibly good. And regardless of your level of experience or interest, you will learn, you will laugh, you will look forward to the next get-together. Guaranteed. So pick up your phone and start inviting some friends. Let the wine work its magic. As it loves to do.

THREE

THREE

USE A SOMMELIER, AT LEAST ONCE, COMPLETELY

N OWADAYS MANY RESTAURANTS, EVEN SMALLER ONES, feature wine lists that include hundreds of offerings from any number and assortment of regions and vintages. It has become the style among too many establishments to flaunt the rare and the obscure, wines with tiny production numbers from regions unfamiliar to all but the cognoscenti. Hidden among such mysterious listings—which seldom include even basic information like the grape variety or varieties involved—are some marvelous bottlings. Yet how many among us, partisans of the good stuff included, would know what to expect from a Segesta Golfo del Tigullio or a Coutandin Pinerolese Ramie?

At the other end of the spectrum are the lists composed of eight Chardonnays, four Sauvignon Blancs, a Riesling or two, a dozen Pinot Noirs, a handful of Merlots, two handfuls of Cabernet Sauvignons and a smattering of Malbecs, Sangioveses, or Syrahs.

Minus detailed descriptions—in other words, in most cases—it's next to impossible to tell which Cab is classically structured, which is showing a distinct vegetal note, and which may be sapid with flavors of blackberry, tobacco, and cassis. Or which Chard is oaked to the point of tasting like butterscotch and which is clean and tight and displaying an elegant restraint. While the advent of new and lesser-known wines appearing on restaurant wine lists is a welcome progression, without explanatory notes—a failure of most lists—we're left in the dark.

It's usually possible to find something familiar, a name or region that rings a bell and that will probably be a serviceable match with the food to be ordered. Truth be told, that's how most folks deal with that difficult-to-decipher list they have been handed. But our mission is to love wine more, not to be confused by it.

Oh, my. What's a body to do?

Well … there is someone who knows every wine on that list. Not the waiter and not the waitress, though they may be pleasant and attempt to be helpful. But if you're lucky and if you're dining in a quality establishment, there's quite possibly a true expert in the house. And this chapter is about leveraging that individual's knowledge for your benefit.

The term is *sommelier*, sometimes an official designation, as in Master Sommelier or Certified Sommelier, and sometimes not. But anyone so declared is a person who has studied, tasted, assessed, and evaluated thousands of wines. This is a true lover of juice, a student of all things vinous. A geek's geek, a devotee of Dionysius, and occasionally, a pompous pain in the ass who's forgotten that the main objective is to share and excite, not pontificate or impress. Thankfully, the stuffed-shirt variety is a dwindling breed, giving way to a younger, less uptight, more freewheeling version. Still, many folks are decidedly unwilling to take the chance, for fear of encountering the old-school attitude and snobbery.

But just for an exceptionally good time, just to lie back on the sun-splattered raft of life and let the current take you where it will, just for the luxury of off-loading the choice to someone else—someone eminently qualified—and just for the fun and experience of observing a specialized vocation at its highest level, seek out the restaurant's sommelier, or wine director or steward, as he or she may be called.

Any somm worth her weight in crushed grapes can tell you more than you need to know about the world's major regions, most of the minor ones, what grapes are used in just about anything put into a bottle, how those grapes and wines should and do taste, and what their flavors and aromas tell you about the wine, including its age and origins, and quite possibly the philosophy of its winemaker. Sounds crazy, but it's true.

This means even an average sommelier is an absolute wealth of knowledge. And as a customer of the restaurant, you get to use and enjoy the benefits of that experience, of all that study and enthusiasm, at no additional cost. With or without the advice of, direction from, and/or conversation with a sommelier, the wine price remains the same. Back in the day, somms wore a *tastevin*, a shallow cup of hammered silver, on a chain around their necks to quickly assess the color, clarity, quality, and aromas of a wine they were about to serve. You'll seldom see a tastevin swinging from its chain anymore, such displays of near-liturgical dress having fallen from favor in this age of democratization, but any upscale restaurant worth its seasoning will field at least a single wine expert among its front-of-the-house staff. Even the least of these, my fellow acolytes, can be well worth engaging.

Objective No. 1 is to enjoy your evening. Objective No. 2 is to expand your experience in the wonderful world of wine. Pretend you're seeing a brilliant new movie or a play or show that has all your friends tweeting its virtues. There's no need to be the director; instead, sit back and play the role of happy but discerning audience. Here's a chance to let someone else work for, and entertain, you and your fellow diners.

Begin thus: *Excuse me, is there a sommelier here, someone who can help us with the wine?*

An excellent start, though one we geeks may find hard to initiate. To our own detriment, we hate to give up control over the wine selection process. But just once, chillax and be smarter than that.

We'd like some assistance choosing a wine. And we're open to trying something new.

Have an idea how much you'd like to spend. Talk with your tablemates about the food and get a sense of what will be ordered. Be prepared to articulate some info about your general wine preferences—which could be as basic as liking a particular style or varietal, and not knowing much about any others, or as detailed as favoring Rioja Reservas over Gran Reservas because their more robust mouthfeel, along with some lingering fruit, is more to your palate than the aged, woody, caramel notes of the older wine.

Whatever your level of comfort or familiarity, whether you're a newcomer to the halls of maceration or an old hand, a capable somm is trained to ferret out your inclinations and match them with your menu selections. You might be asked if you take your coffee black or with cream and sugar or whether you're a person who routinely salts his or her food. Sounds odd, but there's a method to this crazy questioning. Play along. Laugh, smile, enjoy; remember, the burden's on them to maximize your wine pleasure for the evening.

Most sommeliers, in addition to being true wine lovers, are decidedly convivial. You'll find them to be intelligent, well-traveled, and ready conversationalists. The good ones—i.e., the majority—are a pleasure to chat with. The real fun is when they pinpoint two or three wine possibilities for your consideration, none of which you know or have heard of, and the reasoning behind their selections.

Use them here to expand your own body of wine knowledge. Ask more about the grape type they've chosen or the region where it was grown and produced. What would they compare it to? Is this a wine or wine type that's widely available, should you be interested in purchasing the same style or variety in the future? As with all consultative relationships, there is an element of trust required here. But if you're not sold, press for details. How would they compare the first option with the second? Is there another wine similar to these that's a bit less costly? And then pick one. Remember, the objective is to be open and enjoy something new, to wriggle your toes a bit deeper into the sands of the vine, to enlist the somm's assistance as your for-tonight-only guide and mentor.

A quick point: when your sommelier steps away to procure the chosen bottle, sniff the wine glass that your server has set out. It should smell clean and neutral, not like bleach or detergent. Unfortunately, in some restaurants the dish-washing equipment does an inadequate job of rinsing glassware. If your glass smells like a swimming pool, it will ruin the wine. Ask for another.

When your wine guru returns, observe how she presents the bottle, label out, for confirmation that it's what you ordered, as well as her technique for cutting the capsule and removing the cork. She may place the cork on the table for your inspection. This element of the ritual has a dual rationale: first, as all wine corks are stamped or printed with the name of the winery and often the vintage, it's a consumers' guarantee that what's in the bottle is what the label claims and not a counterfeit (an unlikely scenario unless you've ordered a rare and pricey trophy wine). Second, should a wine stain, a streak of color, run the length of the cork, the seal may have been compromised and the wine exposed to oxygen. You won't know until you sample it, but it's a warning to pay attention.

Your somm will pour you a small taste. Sniff and sip, not to ascertain how much you like the wine but to assure that it's sound, without obvious defects. A wine that smells of sulfur or wet cardboard may be faulty. Should that be the case, and it does happen, though not often, ask her to try it as well. Everyone in the wine business has to deal with the occasional bad bottle; it's not a big deal, and she will quickly replace it or suggest an alternative if that was the last bottle in the house.

Now, after all the fun and frivolity, you have the pleasure of sipping a wine that's brand-new to you. After learning about the grapes it's made from and the region where it's produced. This is the payoff. How much more engaging than simply picking another Pinot or Chardonnay that you already know. You may choose to forgo utilizing a sommelier every time you're dining in a better restaurant, but now and again—or at least once—enjoy what these wine pros have to offer. After all, they just want to share their knowledge and enthusiasm with others who love wine as much as they do.

4

FOUR
FOUR

THROW AWAY THE STEMLESS GLASSES

S TEMLESS GLASSES? GET RID OF THEM. DONATE THOSE questionable quaffers to whoever wants them. It's true that wine has been drunk from the hollowed-out trunks of saplings, from fire-hardened mugs made of clay or mud, from stone bowls and sewn-together animal skins. But, we no longer live in the Neolithic.

A lot of wine events, mass tastings, etc., like to hand out stemless glasses; they're easy to make, easy to pack, easy to ship, and portend to lessen the "formality" or "snobbery" of wine. A laudable goal. They may be good for the event organizers, and not terrible for the attendees: however, they're far from ideal when it comes to maximizing a drinkers' enjoyment.

Glasses have undergone their own evolution, and it's well-established that a tulip-shaped bowl directs a wine's volatile components, i.e., its aromas, its sensual essence, to a confined area at the opening of the glass, one easily accessed by a probing, err ... proboscis. Likewise, the art or act of tasting wine has changed as well. Instead of merely passing a silver goblet under one's schnoz en route to sucking down the vessel's contents, modern winos are enamored of the see, swirl, sniff, etc., etc., school of vinous appreciation. And for good reason.

Drinkers of days gone by enjoyed the smell and taste of wine and delighted in the loosening of tongues and strictures and the resultant escalation of social interaction. As might be imagined, today's oenophiles seek a more complete experience. And who can deny that wine is a beautiful thing when gazed upon—bright, clean and rich in color, how gorgeous that limpid ruby or that golden yellow hue—through clear and polished glass? So, unlike those emperors and empresses of yore, today's drinkers can view their wine with crystalline, clear-as-a-bell transparency. Examine it before tasting, marveling at the hue and intensity; gaze upon it, sparkling and colorful in countenance; explore its clarity and observe the light dancing through it. Hence, we see.

How important this vision is, especially when enjoying and responding to a wonderful red wine. The color alone plucks strings in the instrument of our most hidden selves. Through both physiological and societal evolution, humans have progressed from seeing the world only in black and white and shades of gray to modern humankind's ability to distinguish literally thousands of colors in the subtlest of variations. But the first color on that path, for all people in all parts of the world, at all times in history was red. Our ability to distinguish red is our most ancient color-recognition triumph. Even today, there is no color with the power or complex messaging of red.

Red means aggression and strength; it speaks to passion and sex and warns of dangers to be avoided and of blood spilled, of the very essence of life. Wine's association with blood is as old as wine itself and grabs at our primordial hearts, our deepest hopes and fears. Wine and blood have intermingled as offerings to gods and goddesses since the beginnings of worship. This is no mere liquid you are learning to love; it is a life force, a symbol of renewal, of fertility, of humankind's communion and relationship with the almighty.

The steps of the tasting ritual are intended to more fully acquaint you with the precious elixir in your glass. Thanks to the shape and the very convenient handle, i.e., the stem of a wineglass, it becomes an easy matter to spin and whirl the glass, to cause a miniature whirlpool of red or white to rise up along the inside of the bowl, to coat the surface with a revealing layer of wine before it settles back down to a flat, calm surface. Being no more than a few molecules thick and fully exposed to the air, that freshly deposited coating quickly evaporates, lifting the volatile aromatic compounds and sending them forth, hopefully into waiting nostrils to tell their tale. Hence, we swirl and sniff.

Next, whatever the vessel, we swallow. Unless tasting as a wine professional for business purposes, in which case we spit. And then, in either case, we savor. So there you have it, according to the customs and capabilities of the times: see, swirl, sniff, swallow and savor. Each step uncovering more of the mystery in our glass, and strengthening our connection to it. While you're free to drink wine from whatever vessel you choose: a tin cup, a coffee mug, a promotional water bottle covered with text and logos advertising an insurance agency or sports team, or even from a Styrofoam cup, you will be denying yourself the full experience of pleasure and denying your wine the respect it has been accorded since time immemorial.

As you are prone to do with a stemless glass. Oh, sure, you can see the wine—until smudges of grease or oil from your fingers have clouded the glass and impaired visibility. You like your wine at a certain temperature? Cooler for whites, not quite so cool for reds? How about wrapping a hand around the glass and warming it beyond its appropriate temperature? Thank you, stemless.

Then, should you wish to swirl, to smell and sniff and ponder the multitude of messaging that a wine's aromas send forth: grape variety, source, age, winemaking style, etc., you'll find that it's an awkward exercise with a stemless glass, resembling the vinous equivalent of a sippy cup.

With all due respect to the distinguished family of glass makers whose creative heir-designate devised these insidious containers, banish them from your wine cabinet, for they do you no favors.

It's true that stemless glasses can and do have a place. They are wonderful for lemonade or iced tea, with their not-displeasing roly-poly shape. And it must be conceded that should you own and entertain on a boat, the silly little things will probably tip over less often in rolling waters, thereby saving both wine and white-clad, wine-drinking guests from unnecessary spillage.

And when in Rome.... Many a wonderful meal has been enjoyed in the Italian countryside, a marvelous lunch under the dazzling summer sun or a plate of scrumptious prosciutto and Parmesan overlooking another of Tuscany or Piemonte or Sicily's idyllic vistas. The wine poured, so often, into tumblers of pressed glass, fun and funky with nary a stem in sight. And how delicious it is! Yet this is more about wine's ability to enhance a situation, to be part of local lore and custom, to remind us that there's a time and place for everything, than an endorsement of less-than-optimal glassware.

Drink from stems; enjoy, appreciate, and give cred to the lovely liquid therein. Be a stalwart. Be thankful and show appreciation to the gods of wine, to Bacchus and Dionysius. Pour, observe, marvel, and savor. Welcome to the troupe.

HOT DOG AND ITALIAN WHITE

THE DIVERSITY OF WINE IS STUNNING. THERE'S A WINE NOT merely to pair with just about any food imaginable but a particular bottling of juice from somewhere, made by someone, that's able to transform your food and wine into a synergistic medley of gustatory nirvana. Anyone who eats and drinks and appreciates a happy palate can confirm that this is the case.

From flavors of blackberry, cedar, and black pepper to fresh pears drizzled with honey—and everything in between—it's hard to imagine a taste, be it sweet or savory, that's not represented on the spectrum of sensations that wine delivers. That said, food and wine pairing remains more art than science. And just because there's a perfect wine for every food doesn't mean it's easily found.

Much that we read about food and wine pairing is pure bunk. The majority of proffered combos are no more than a truce: the food is good, the wine is good, and they don't interfere with each other.

Some pairings are downright nasty, detrimental to both parties. And some are sublime, heavenly, making the food taste better than it's ever tasted and revealing the wine's direct connection to the gods.

A problem is that people fall back on "rules" to determine the exemplary match. Yet for every such rule, any oenophile can produce famous, much-beloved pairings that totally undermine these superficial decrees. The complexity of the task far outweighs the simplicity of fixed guidelines. The variables are everywhere, and all parties to the interaction bring them in spades.

The food: well-prepared or not so deftly handled; high, searing heat or low and slow. The protein: corn- or grass-fed, farmed or fished, free range or caged. The vegetables: picked early or late, this variety or that. The seasonings ... well, you get the point.

But all that uncertainty is just as characteristic of the wine: one vintage or another; used oak or new, or none at all; hillside vineyards or grown on the flat; this clone or that or yet another; sustainable or biodynamic; interventionist or not.

You begin to realize that broad pronouncements approach uselessness.

And then comes the most variable of all: the diner. The person. The palate. The proclivities. The preferences. The memories. The associations. He loves what you hate. Pickles make one person gag while another devours them by the jarful; this one adores tuna, that one despises it. Each to his own, said the old lady ... again, you get the point.

In such complex multi-variable systems, it's often serendipity that trumps chaos. The accidental discovery, the hand-me-down nugget of wisdom, the random occurrence.

Wait! Stop! Isn't this a book about loving wine? Why all the gobbledygook about chaos and complexity? Where are the hot dogs?

You're right. Forgive me the digression. And by way of explanation, the hot dogs are right here, ready to be enjoyed along with a tasty and remarkable wine pairing recently unearthed at the intersection of accidental discovery and random occurrence. Even better, it seems that any style of dog works. Wonderfully. Grilled, boiled, all-beef, red hots; Chicago-style with sliced tomato, sport peppers and celery salt; New York dogs topped with kraut and brown mustard; Southern-style buried in coleslaw; Coneys, Sonoran, even Chilean *completos* or Colombian *perros calientes.*

And the mystery wine accompaniment (for those who've yet to read the chapter title) that makes this pairing a match to remember? A veritable bouquet of Italian whites, any one of which makes a dog howl with delight. There's something about the clean, lean, crisp and muted flavors of Italian white wines that pays homage to the entire hot dog family of encased meats.

These wines are dry, medium- to light-bodied, often minerally with a dash of fresh-cut herbs, a suggestion of sea breeze, a touch of citrus or white flower notes, maybe a hint of quince and a fluttering of bitter almond. Acidity that cuts yet respects the condiments and brings the dog front and center.

There is a wonderful back-and-forth between these two, as if the hot dog says, "Please, you take the applause," but the wine will have none of that. "Oh, no," it replies, "it's you they want. Take a bow, my friend, well-deserved."

Such class, such professionalism. Get yourself a ticket for this show as soon as possible. And look for productions co-starring Verdicchio of Marche, Orvieto of Umbria, or Pecorino d'Abruzzo (yes, pecorino is a cheese, too, named for *pecora*, the sheep that enjoy grazing on these selfsame, lovely grapes). You might also locate a production with Ribolla Gialla of Friuli, Vermentino of Sardinia, or, should Dionysus be smiling—how fitting that Dionysus is the god of both wine *and* theater—Fiano, Falanghina or Greco di Tufo, all with long ties to Campania.

Others have tried to pull this role off, but the subtleties, the quiet nuance, the give-and-take elude most players. The Piemontese cousins, Arneis and Gavi, came close, their efforts admirable but the former a bit fruity and the latter too flowery. Soave of Veneto, a real peach, was likewise considered, but rich yellow fruit proved to be a less complimentary addition to this remarkable ensemble.

Here we truly have a case of eat, drink, and be much enamored of the combination. Hot dogs and Italian whites—that's a performance everyone's gotta love. So get your tickets now!

6

SIX

SIX

FIND YOUR FAVORITE

T
HE PRESCRIPTION "TO LOVE WINE MORE" IMPLIES A SELF-
awareness of what you love and know about wine right now.
There is no common, anointed path one should follow. Every
wine drinker embarks on a unique journey. We take sustenance from
one another's impressions and experiences when and as we can, but
no two enthusiasts begin or end in the same place.

Much like establishing a baseline in any dynamic situation, a
starting point from which to measure and assess future advances or
permutations, it's helpful to isolate and identify ground zero for the
would-be fan of fermented beverage.

And it's fun. Gather together a sampling of the wines you think
you're most attracted to. If you favor big reds, scoop up a variety
of candidates. For someone who has enjoyed Cabernet Sauvignons,
for example, the selection might include a left bank Bordeaux, a
Chilean Cab, a Napa Cab, a Cabernet from the Columbia Valley in

Washington state, perhaps a Cab-dominant Super Tuscan, and a Cabernet Sauvignon from South Africa.

Just to be sure, include a smattering of other big reds. A Syrah from the northern Rhone, another from Australia or Chile, maybe a Priorat from Spain or a red blend from the Douro in northern Portugal. Since it's always more enjoyable to drink with others, get on the horn and have your friends come by to sip and share. You might even decide to taste all these wines blind if you have someone who can bag them.

But there's no need to hurry. A leisurely pace spread over multiple tastings works just fine. A few samples this week and few more next week achieves the goal just as well. Most folks find it kind of exciting to pinpoint which wines they most enjoy, but you shouldn't think it has to be done in a single sitting.

One approach that works well if you have friends who likewise enjoy the mystical juice is to announce a tasting and ask everyone to bring a good bottle of, following our example, Cabernet from somewhere out of the ordinary. (In this way you won't get half a dozen Napa Cabs and nothing else.) It spreads the cost and allows you the chance to pick up those Syrahs and perhaps a Merlot or two. Or if light reds are more to your liking, consider instead a selection of Pinot Noirs, Beaujolais, or Dolcettos.

You're more into medium-bodied whites? Then how about a medley of lightly oaked Chardonnays, a couple Sauvignon Blancs, one of those lovely Italians discussed in the previous chapter, and maybe a Sémillon or a Pinot Gris from Oregon?

Whoa! Before we get too far, let's admit that some drinkers may have never tried a Sémillon or know which Chardonnays are minimally oaked and which are not. Fair enough. So, two points. One is that a good retailer is an invaluable source of guidance and information. Stop by your favorite, or newly discovered, wine shop and ask for recommendations. A knowledgeable wine seller will be delighted to assist. Pick some brains; it's the accepted thing to do. If everyone comes into a store and knows exactly what he or she wants, life gets very boring for the poor wine retailer.

Two is that long-time drinkers, be they in the wine trade or not, have probably tasted enough wines from enough regions that they have effectively completed this exercise and are well along on their own oenological evolution. Lucky them. Of course, they'd still love to join your tasting; any excuse to enjoy something they haven't tried in a while is always welcome, and they'll probably bring a good bottle. But for the average love-to-love-wine-more budding connoisseur, it's both satisfying and instructive to see what your palate favors at this point. So let's get to it, shall we?

You might consider dividing your candidate wines into flights of three or four. It's easier to compare fewer wines at once. You may go through two or three flights, or four or five, depending entirely on the intensity of your interest and the size of your pocketbook. Whatever works, works. Remember, there is no right or wrong path, no single approach to wine or its appreciation. We aren't interested in spending money or making a statement; we're having a good time and learning how to love a greater part of our human culture and history.

Sip and taste and compare and contrast and discuss and consider the wines you have poured. Which ones please you? And which pleases you most? If you don't know the wines you're trying, just pour, taste, and evaluate. If you do know them, or some of them, or if you think one region is superior to another, you're better off tasting the wines blind. The power of suggestion is huge and very able to skew objective impressions. Just knowing that a wine is from your favored region or from a famous winery can cause you to perceive it as being better than if you tasted the same wine "in the dark," without knowing who makes it or where it's from.

Get some bags. Ask the wine seller for a handful of those tall brown paper wine-bottle bags. They are ideal for blind tasting; just put each bottle in a bag and wrap a length of tape around the top.

Mix them up or let someone else determine the pouring order. Focus on what's in your glass, not the labels inside the bags.

It's great fun to taste blind, especially when the only objective is to choose which wine you like the best. It's not about guessing vintages or varieties or regions or producers. It's solely, and entirely, about choosing which wine you prefer. And only you can make that determination.

There's something intriguing, comforting in a way, to say to yourself—based on tasting, not guessing—that at this point in your vinous sojourn, Barbera—Italian Barberas, to be precise—are your favorite wines. Or that Cabernet Sauvignons, from Chile or from Coonawarra, in Australia, are the wines you enjoy the most. You may

Wine bottles bagged for blind tasting

have discovered that you'll get the greatest pleasure and bang for your rupees from buying a Pinot Grigio from Alsace or a Viognier from Washington state the next time you make a wine purchase. Or a Beaujolais from Morgon or a Tempranillo from Ribera del Duero.

The only one to please is you. This kind of tasting is solely for the purpose of helping you recognize and remember the wine type or variety you enjoy the most. Other opinions matter not. Some will agree with you, many will not. But the focus here is to identify your

Mmmm. A nose of yellow apple, pear and ... what is that?

favorite, which in turn grounds you in the world of wine and puts you in the perfect place from which to begin the rest of your journey down the long and winding river of Dionysus' delights.

SEVEN
SEVEN

REALIZE THAT YOUR FAVORITES WILL CHANGE CONSTANTLY

N OW THAT YOU'VE FOUND THE WINE YOU MOST LOVE TO drink, let go. Realize that your tastes and preferences will change. I used to love Bordeaux above all others; I love them still, though I drink them less often. I once took pleasure in the unctuous, butterscotch quality of heavily oaked California Chardonnay; these days I've lost my taste for such wines and now prefer a more natural, expressive approach, to white grapes especially. Big jammy Australian fruit bombs, Shiraz for the most part, at one time provided me with great pleasure, but now I lean more toward elegance and restraint.

But my journey is just that—mine. And your journey will be yours. What delights you is wonderful, what doesn't is best left for another day. As we age, our tastes change. We experience a new flavor or a new texture and are drawn to it. Such is the beauty of wine. Nothing is forever; we learn, we experience, we advance, and we learn anew.

There is no fixed path. I love wine more because it offers flavors I have yet to encounter from regions I have yet to explore. What a rush, for instance, to experience the magnificence of Moschofilero, a Greek white that makes me wonder what I ever saw in a simple Chardonnay. Or a Grechetto from central Italy that reinforces everything that Moschofilero offered on our first meeting.

Learning to love wine is learning to accept the plenitude that you have yet to experience, and trusting that it awaits you. There is nothing cautionary here, merely a heads-up that wine has ten thousand years of permutations to share, versus your ten or twenty or forty years of indulgence. It's all in your favor; you're guaranteed a magnificent journey ahead. Wine is a remarkable beverage. It has been part of human existence for thousands of years, since before the end of the Ice Age and well before the domestication of plants or animals. Our relationship with wine is complex and multi-layered; it is both symbol and object and has played supporting roles in most of the drama that is human and social evolution.

To put it more simply, the wine you love today will probably be replaced by another—sooner rather than later. This is how it should be. It has nothing to do with a "maturing palate" (a rather condescending construct) but everything to do with a deeper, more thorough exploration of grape juice fermented and presented for your pleasure and acceptance.

A significant part of wine appreciation involves an understanding of context. For example, you would probably not be enamored of a sweet, oxidized white from southern Italy, say a Greco or Falanghina (still available in a dry style), until you realize that this was quite possibly the celebrated *Falernian* of ancient Rome, lauded by Pliny the Elder and renowned throughout the ancient world. This wine's remarkable vintage of 121 BC was served to Caesar in 60 BC, sixty-one years after harvest, to celebrate his conquest of

Spain. Are you kidding me? I'd drink that wine anytime, anywhere, just for the experience.

There is always more; there is never an end to what you've not yet tasted. It's wonderful to try and compare, to challenge the wine, to ask that it show us what excellent grapes from a specific terroir can do when handled with care and respect. This chapter portends no great lesson; it is rather an acknowledgement that the curiosity of our tastes combined with the panoply of wines produced serves our palates well. Drink a lot. Drink many wines. Enjoy them. Envision men and women and groups of oenophiles sipping the self-same wines two or three or four thousand years ago. That is the evolution. Love wine. It has much to offer.

EIGHT
EIGHT

INTRODUCE A BEER-DRINKING FRIEND TO WINE

B EER AND WINE ARE HISTORIC COHORTS, A HAPPY TWOSOME
that's been around since the late (or Upper) Paleolithic age.
Children of serendipity, as both were undoubtedly "accidental" discoveries, they have together quenched thirsts, provided
sustenance, and lubricated deistic festivities from the fertile crescent to the far ends of the earth. Leading lights of the fraternity of
fermentation, they might be called.

We've recently seen beer drinkers split into two camps: those
pleased by and loyal to an old familiar friend, the style or brand they've
enjoyed for years, and those who have embraced the emergence of
craft beer with its many variations. The former ensconce a particular
brew in their shrine of comfort and routine, habituated as they are to
the congeniality of recognition. Craft brew advocates, however, find

Cheers to both the gorgeous brews.

less satisfaction with the old-school approach and much prefer beer and ale made with a certain reverence for the best of European tradition married with New World innovation and devil-may-care insouciance—which in some cases results in a magnificent expression of the brewers' art while, in others, merely provides an overwrought example of fermented grains adulterated with adjuncts gone wild.

But beer, however refreshing, is not our focus. It is wine that we love and things vinous that excite our palates. Grape juice bubbling in the throes of fermentation brings solace to our hearts, and such simple yet profound pleasure we need share with our grainy brethren and sistren, for surely then all the days of our, and their, lives shall be enriched with the sipping, the tasting, and the enjoyment of fine wine.

Few among the ranks of wine drinkers shy from the pleasure of an occasional IPA, pilsner, or stout, yet the sweet luxury of our own favored elixir is too often foreign to followers of the barley brew. There is no good reason for this state beyond lack of opportunity or introduction. Our world of plump thin-skinned berries wields great power and can be, at times, difficult to decipher. Which is where you and I and all our ilk need to come together. By teaching and sharing our insights, by offering our guidance and clearing a way into the wonders of wine for our beery comrades, we achieve two noble goals.

First, we gather our oenological thoughts, assess the breadth and worth of our information, and reflect on the many experiences enjoyed while sampling the beloved juice. Don't be concerned if you're a newcomer to the creed; a reckoning of this sort will show how much more you know than you may have thought. Besides, it's not the technical details or a clever recitation of styles and varieties that's required. It's simply the oomph, the friendly nudge of your personal sparkle and encouragement that will bring a sip and a swallow of some lovely wine to the lips of our beer-centric companions.

Second, there is no greater expression of one's growing love for wine than to share it with others. Wine is a social animal; it revels in being part of a group, in stimulating conversation and bringing smiles and laughter to all those gathered round. You may have noticed how wine invites others to join in your conclave: drinkers nearby, neighbors, friends of friends, whether in the local pub, at a backyard barbecue, or out for an evening of good cheer.

The secret to beguiling your brew buddies is to first think about what they drink, not what you drink or what you'd like them to drink. It's a sharing you're after, not a conversion. The concept is to make everyone welcome, even if their wine consumption is only an occasional event involving no more than a glass or two.

At parties, dinners, etc., a sure sign of hospitality is to offer your guests some well-chosen beer alongside whatever wines have been selected for the occasion. Strive to make no one feel unwelcome or overlooked. Remember, good winos are good company, and we should address the comfort and cheer of all. It is, unfortunately, unusual to be offered a Belgian dubbel or a pale ale at the same venue that's featuring the wines of Piemonte or Stellenbosch or the Rattlesnake Hills. Be the host everyone wishes for but seldom encounters. Break the mold and win the hearts of all your guests, be they fellow wine lovers or beer drinkers still dabbling at the edges of the crimson pool.

And when offering wine to those folks most enamored of amber gulps of grain, do so with a wine that makes sense vis-à-vis their palate and not your convenience. To wit, if you enjoy lazing by the pool with a chilled glass of Pinot Grigio, don't think you'll win over your Strong Scotch Ale-drinking buddy with a glass of the same. On the flip side of that particular bottle cap, attempting to entice the light lager drinker with a high-alcohol, in-your-face Zinfandel is most assuredly a futile pursuit.

As the author of *A Beer Drinker's Guide To Knowing And Enjoying Fine Wine*, I'm often asked if there is a simple key to selecting an appropriate wine for the average beer drinker, perhaps along the lines of color-matching with their usual brew, i.e., white wine for lager drinkers, big reds for stout and porter fans. At first blush, that sounds fairly reasonable, but what this approach overlooks is that many dark beers, for example, are characterized by lower alcohol levels and a distinct touch of sweetness, a very different expectation than one has of most inky, deep-hued wines. Or that a rather light-colored, innocent-looking IPA can be as bitter as a young Barolo is tannic.

A better starting point, I discovered only through much trial and fuzzy contemplation, is to consider the intensity of the actual drinking experience. By that I mean to say an easy-going, medium- to low-alcohol pilsner or pale ale might be pleasingly exchanged for a less fruity Old World Chardonnay like a Petit Chablis or a

Pouilly-Fuissé. Both beer and wines are smooth and enjoyable while being fairly neutral, not overwhelming in body, alcohol, or flavor intensity, able to quietly accompany food or conversation in a supporting role.

Or consider instead a saison, a beer that dances in your mouth and insists on being noticed. It's not the biggest, not the richest or most powerful of the brewer's lineup, but it certainly has presence and personality. A fitting wine to offer a fan of saisons or farmhouse ale in general is one that mirrors the qualities that define these complex, fruity, spicy, earthy, higher-alcohol brews, and what comes to mind is a dirty, fruity product of the southern Rhone, showcasing Grenache and Syrah with a touch of Mourvèdre, Cinsault or Counoise; in other words, a Côtes du Rhône or, if you have a few more shekels to rub together, a Vacqueyras, Gigondas, Rasteau, or Cairanne, former Côtes du Rhône appellations stepped up to their own AOCs (*Appellations d'Origine Contrôlée*).

One can almost imagine a saison and a Côtes du Rhône becoming friends, meeting for drinks in some little out-of-the-way bar in the backwaters of rural Belgium or southern France, remarking on their similarities and ending the night with arms flung around each other's shoulders, stumbling out the door, and swearing eternal fealty.

The point, though, is that neither would be enamored of a witbier or a Trebbiano. Bring your barley-centric friends into the wine fold—if not as aficionados, at least as appreciators—by offering them a version of wine their palates can relate to. They'll be pleasantly surprised, and you will have done all winedom a welcome service.

Following is a list of style pairings, beer to wine, based on similarities of mouthfeel, complexity, power, and presence. A rough guide, to be sure, but a starting point nonetheless. And after all, it's about fun and sharing and social lubrication, and only a fool would try to make it more.

Favorite Beer Style	May Enjoy This White Wine	May Enjoy This Red Wine
Light Lager	Muscadet	Valpolicella
Pilsner/Vienna Lager	Vinho Verde	Dolcetto
Weisse/Witbier	Albariño	Beaujolais
Wheat Beer	Riesling	Rioja Crianza
Pale Ale	Chablis	Chianti
Brown Ale	Verdejo	Nero d'Avola
Amber Ale/Red Ale	Soave	Cabernet Franc
Saison	Sauvignon Blanc	Grenache
English Bitter	Chenin Blanc	Sagrantino
Dubbel	Chardonnay	Pinot Noir
Bock/Dunkel	Pinot Gris	Merlot
IPA	Grüner Veltliner	Nebbiolo
Scotch Ale	Moschofilero	Syrah
Belgian Strong Ale	Gewürztraminer	Malbec
Porter/Stout	Sémillon	Bordeaux
Barleywine	Marsanne	Priorat

The list is hardly exhaustive—brewers groups and beer competitions routinely include a hundred or more delineated styles—but it covers much of what's drunk on a daily basis. And to be honest, twenty interested onlookers might come up with twenty variations. But again, that misses the point. There is no final, exact correlation; give a beer drinker a wine with a combination of weight, alcohol, flavors, and complexity that suggest his or her regular draught and you will have done your job. There's no controlling another drinker's palate—you can only offer what you hope they will enjoy. And by following these guidelines, many will. Prost!

9

NINE
NINE

DRINK, AND SERVE, FROM MAGNUMS

THERE'S A WONDERFUL CELEBRATORY QUALITY TO LARGE-
format bottles. They enhance the wine experience on many
levels. Think of ancient amphorae being emptied into kraters, of tuxedoed hosts letting fly the corks from Jeroboams of
Champagne, of you hosting a dinner party for guests wide-eyed at
the sight of festive oversize bottles waiting to be poured.

Their very presence shouts, "Welcome! Enter here and enjoy.
You're valued at this table, and we're glad that you've joined us."

Magnums, with double the fun of a regular wine bottle, are as
much a sign of hospitality as were fresh pineapples mounted atop
fence posts outside the homes of colonial seafarers, and proclaim
nearly the same thing: we've been abroad and have returned with
exotic goods to share with friends and neighbors.

There is no better wine to serve at a gathering of people who are important to you than that which flows from a large bottle. Snickers of surprised delight, unmuted oohs and aahs, are the standard utterings of guests at the sight of big bottles anxious to be drained and join the party. Magnum, Jeroboam, Rehoboam, Methuselah, Salmanazar and so on (depending on availability both of a particular bottle size and of sufficient funds in your account to make the purchase). In order listed, these babies hold two, four, six, eight, or twelve times the contents of a standard 750 ml wine bottle—and they stand proud and tall on the table, sentinels, servants of Dionysus, harbingers of an evening of pleasure, of chatting and laughter, of challenge and confirmation.

Magnums are the most *simpatico* to pour from, large enough to impress yet still easy to handle. The generosity of spirit, the *joie de vivre* of it all, causes one's thoughts to drift from the symposia of postprandial Greece to the salons of nineteenth century Paris.

Take a look around the next time you visit a good wine shop. Magnums and other large size bottles are frequently to be had at less expense than expected. It is always a good idea to have two or three of these generous bottles in reserve, ready to draw gasps of pleasure from your invitees. Don't be tempted by mediocrity in a big bottle; plenty of delicious wines are routinely offered in larger format.

If you have not yet experienced the physical, tangible,

Champagne Drappier from large to small

and tactile exhilaration of serving your guests from a magnum, let me assure you that it's worth the time and the expenditure. The sight of bright eyes and smiling faces appreciating what for many is a unique moment—think about that, *what for many is a unique moment*—is a delectable point from which to begin an evening of Bacchanalian jubilation.

Take it, the evening and the revelry, where you will. Excess and unbridled cheer are frequent companions. In days past, consumption of wine in copious amounts was an obligation to the gods. Societies through the ages have considered drunken celebration a connection, a conduit, to the everlasting. While such ritualized overindulgence is best consigned to the shadowy alleyways of history, the glow of friendship, relaxation, and good company and conversation, i.e., the "social lubricant" effect of wine is always welcome.

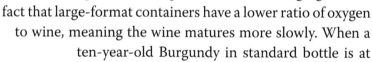

And we've yet to discuss the science of commodious bottles. There is an additional element that adds to the appeal of magnums and their more spacious siblings. It has to do with aging and the fact that large-format containers have a lower ratio of oxygen to wine, meaning the wine matures more slowly. When a ten-year-old Burgundy in standard bottle is at its prime, juice of the selfsame vintage, resting comfortably in large format has years to go before reaching the equivalent level of maturity. Magnums delight, Jeroboams tease, and Salmanazars dare us to a regime of patience. Ah, Bacchus … you bastard. You encourage our consumption and then toy with our sensibilities. May you offer a merrymaker's debauch to us all.

But readiness aside, the true gift of large formats is the sense of generosity they impart to those who offer and share them. We may never reach the heights of power and influence enjoyed by the rulers of antiquity, though by filling our guests' glasses from a seemingly inexhaustible crucible, we can, for a moment, emulate the bounteous gesture of Assyrian King Salmanazar in feting his royal court and honored assembly. Or wonder at the historical import of Nebuchadnezzar, all-powerful king of Babylon, whose namesake bottle holds twenty times that of lesser containers. Here was a man who defeated the Egyptians in battle, conquered Palestine, captured and razed Jerusalem, yet praised the God of Israel and built the wondrous Hanging Gardens of Babylon that his honored wife, Queen Amytis, might not miss the green hills of her Persian homeland. Complex, powerful, and passionate.

It's all this that makes me love wine more. Salud.

LEARN A LITTLE GEOGRAPHY

THERE'S NO NEED TO BECOME A MAESTRO, BUT KNOWING the outlines of global wine geography will stand you in good stead and help fit together pieces of the vinous puzzle. Wine vines and grapes, specifically of the species *Vitis vinifera*, grow comfortably in the temperate climes of 30° to 50° north or south latitude. Too warm and they get fat and lazy and lose their interest; too cool and they turn hard and green and lose their appeal. But within these general parameters of north and south, wine vines are in their natural habitat, able to thrive, to grow and flower and produce their sweet and tasty fruit.

Other factors are to be considered as well. A region may be at the limits of these latitudinal guidelines but enjoy particular characteristics that still make successful grape growing possible. For example, a south-facing slope above a river that reflects maximum solar energy onto the vines may have the ability to produce quality wine grapes even though it's too cold or too far north—think the Mosel River of Germany. Or somewhere that's considered too warm may have vineyards situated at higher, cooler altitudes or in seaside valleys where they take relief from ocean fog banks that daily bathe grapes and vines in chilly air—think the Elqui Valley of Chile.

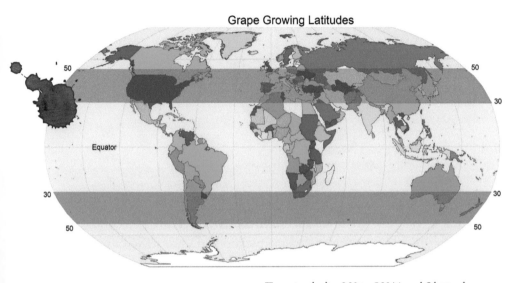

Grape Growing Latitudes

The wine belts: 30° to 50° N and S latitude

These local variations, fog and altitude and aspect of the slope, along with soil types, weather and drainage patterns, diurnal temperature shifts, insect populations, humidity levels, and whether or not field hands are prone to pee on the vines or use portable latrines, all combine to comprise the *terroir* of a specific site. And some, especially the French, believe that terroir is crucial to determining the uniqueness, the idiosyncratic peculiarities, of a given wine.

Others pooh-pooh them.

And yet, a wine vinified of grapes grown in calcareous soil is quite dissimilar to one made from the same grape type grown in sandy soil. A grape that endures constant wind responds with a thickening of the skin, leading to higher phenolic levels in the resulting wines, i.e., deeper colors and more tannins.

Geography, from soil types to general climactic conditions, is a major consideration for both producers and consumers of wine. A Chardonnay from Chablis, a cool climate with chalky, minerally soil, and one from Napa Valley, a warmer climate with richer, more fertile soil, will be vastly different. Which you choose to purchase depends on your personal taste.

Hotter climates typically produce riper fruit. Riper fruit has more sugar, and therefore its wines tend to be higher in alcohol, fuller-bodied, and fatter in the mouth. They also lean in the direction of tropical fruit flavors—pineapple and melon, for example— whereas the cooler climes, like Chablis, produce wines that are leaner, crisper, lower in alcohol, and more likely to show green or yellow apple notes over a minerally base.

Some grape varieties seem more responsive to disparities in terroir than others. Cabernet Sauvignon and Sauvignon Blanc, for instance, acquire distinct vegetal notes when grown in conditions too fertile or too warm or when picked too early. The culprit is a molecular compound known as methoxypyrazine that gives the wine a bell pepper or green herbal flavor. To a large degree, this is desirable in Sauvignon Blanc, but less welcome in Cabernet.

At one point some years ago, pyrazines, as they are called, became almost a signature of Chilean Cabernet Sauvignons. Realizing that extensive vineyard plantings on the fertile valley floors were much to blame, winegrowers began utilizing sites on the slopes and higher ground rising above the valleys, cooler sites with poor soils, less water, and greater challenges for the vines. These new vineyards became the source of markedly improved fruit and rescued Chilean Cabs from the curse of pungent bell pepper flavors and aromas.

Cool versus warm temperatures, whether from routine conditions, higher or lower altitude, seaside breezes or lack thereof, or even vintage variation, have a major impact on the acid level of ready-for-harvest grapes and their resulting wines. Generally

Vines in La Mancha, Spain

speaking, cooler weather keeps acid levels higher. It's acid that gives wine its verve and vibrancy, its liveliness, its mouthwatering aspect. Wines with too little acid will taste dull and heavy, like melted jam, while those with too much will seem sharp and tart, like lemonade in need of sugar.

Terroir is simply geography on a very local scale, physical geography being concerned primarily with site and how the elements of site affect and influence human existence and development. You will hear geographers discuss biogeography, hydrogeography, soils geography, and climatology, all considerations in assessing terroir. In a sense, it can be said that terroir is geography writ small.

One need ask, are these grapes grown in arid regions, where less water equates to greater stress on the plant and tends, therefore, to produce more intense—intensely colored, intensely flavored—grapes, with less pressure from mildew and fungi? Or are they grown in coastal or lowland regions with an excess of water, of humidity, and of the need to be more pro-actively farmed, to have crops and canopies thinned and leaves and roots defended from the dangers of disease and insects?

A basic knowledge of geography is an integral part and vital parcel of the world of wine. Of course one can drink and enjoy wine with no concept of the contours of the vineyard, or of the region, or the latitude, or even of the country of its origin. Look no farther than jugs of blended red or white anchoring the bottom shelves of your local grocery: factory wines bereft of provenance. Drinkable, yes, but our quest here is not merely to consume. It is to enjoy, to engage in, to understand and become one with the past, the present, and the nuances of wine.

On a larger scale, moving beyond the specificity of terroir, beyond the microclimate of individual vines or the mesoclimate of a particular vineyard, we encounter appellation. The terroir, the

Casablanca Valley, Chile

macroclimate of a region, of a stitched-together coverlet of contiguous hills and dales that absorb similar amounts of sunlight and rainfall and cooling fog or desiccating heat. Similar but not exact, yet able to define a geography. Napa, Bordeaux, Piemonte, Alicante, Champagne, Rioja, Victoria, Mendoza, Walla Walla, Central Otago, Colchagua Valley. All have characteristics, peculiarities that influence and define their wines. When you are cognizant of the discrepancies to be expected between a Pinot Noir hailing from the Santa Rita Hills and another from the Côte d'Or you have become a votary of enhanced appreciation.

Knowing what to expect of a wine, and why, based on its place of birth, growth, and vinification is a talent, and a comfort, learned bit by bit, region by region. No one should look to become all-knowing in a single moment. Begin with a grape of interest and explore its typicity, here—there—and somewhere else. It's this kind of earned insight that makes one love wine more, and feel a part of its inner circle.

ELEVEN
ELEVEN

PICK A MONTHLY, OR OCCASIONAL, 'STUDY BUDDY' VARIETY

S ET YOUR SIGHTS ON A SINGLE GRAPE VARIETY OR WINE style; decide, for example, to learn what you can about Malbec or Chianti (the latter usually, though not always, a blend). Do this according to your own schedule: maybe one grape per month, or one every now and then, or one a week, whatever works. The knowledge you gather is immediate, while the overall impact on your "vintellect" is cumulative. A little exploration—be it online, at the local bookstore, or in your favorite wine shop—will yield a surprising amount of information and boost both your confidence and, perhaps more important, the closeness of your relationship with Bacchus.

Malbec in all its glory

Pick up a couple of good generalized books on wine types and varieties. The idea isn't to read them from cover to cover but to flip directly to those sections that discuss Malbec or Chianti or whatever variety or wine you have chosen to learn more about. Do an online search as well; you'll quickly discover which sites offer valuable information and which are simply platforms for sales or advertising.

Believe it or not, many wine grapes have a fascinating history. Malbec, once the darling of Bordeaux, has picked up stakes and moved most of the family to Argentina. How and why and when this happened, and who was left behind and where Malbec is still grown and vinified in its home country, and others, is a story that touches on everything from medieval history to the scourge of phylloxera to the development of high-elevation grape growing. Australia figures into this story, as do Chile, California, and Washington state.

Absorbing this historic panorama (or that of any grape or wine type) will no doubt pique your palate's curiosity and send you straight to the neighborhood wine shop. Poor baby. For that Malbec homework you might want a bottle of Cahors, another from Argentina's Luján de Cuyo and one from the lofty Uco Valley, a selection from the Clare Valley in Australia, something from California, from Napa perhaps—yes, *that* Napa—and don't leave out Walla Walla or the Columbia Valley in Washington or that Chilean entry from Colchagua Valley. Not bad. This is shaping up to be an impressive tasting.

Call the friends. Sniff and swirl and taste and compare. You'll find structures from highly tannic to plush and velvety, colors from near-black to deep ruby to purple magenta. A gorgeous line-up, and with the attendant study you'll know more about Malbec than 90% of the wine drinking world does.

Sangiovese

Viognier

Or that Chianti, the region, best known for the wines of Chianti Classico, is composed of eight separate sub-regions, that Chianti was first described in 1716, that Sangiovese ... well, you get the point. Once you start with this wine-loving stuff, there's no stopping.

Another excellent approach is to assemble a regular tasting group and designate a specific type or varietal of wine as the focus of each get-together. And then rotate the professorial portion of the program from person to person. Next month we're doing Pinot Noir; everyone brings a bottle of Pinot and one person has to provide the research. Styles, terroirs, locales, diversity, history, etc. Maybe even handouts if we're all really into this thing. And maps— why not maps? It is amazingly instructive to sample a Pinot from the Santa Rita Hills next to one from Carneros next to one from Central Otago next to one from northern Italy next to one from the Willamette Valley next to one from Burgundy, whew, and so on. But therein lies the joy.

One Pinot Noir really does not taste like the next, and yet they are all clearly Pinots. Such is the uniqueness of terroir—of soils and weather and rainfall—and of market preferences and regional styles. From dense and fruit-driven to lithe, elegant, and speaking more of tea and spices and nuances of wild berries. They look different, smell different, feel different in the mouth, and most certainly taste different. For most of us, some will have great appeal while others may be less compelling. And with our newfound awareness of those all-important influences, we now know why—a very satisfying outcome. Wine is so much tastier when you know the whys and wherefores, when you're part of the millennia-old community.

Once you've developed a comfort level and familiarity with a variety, you'll be surprised at your new interest in and ability to anticipate what's in the bottle and select that wine, whether in a restaurant or wine store. From there it's an easy matter to choose the next target of your curiosity and start building a portfolio of "wine smarts" that will be with you for life.

Don't overlook the obscure grapes. It's easy to focus on the so-called "noble varieties" simply because these are the varieties most frequently encountered. The reds—Pinot Noir, Cabernet Sauvignon, Merlot, and Syrah—and the whites—Riesling, Chardonnay, and Sauvignon Blanc—are a shape-shifting group that may or may not include Chenin Blanc, Sémillon, and others, red or white, depending on who is doing the listing. This group of predominantly French grapes was accorded the now little-used designation because they consistently produce high-quality wines and are rather easy to grow wherever planted. But to consider a Merlot or a Cabernet more "noble" than a Nebbiolo, a Tempranillo, or a Nero d'Avola is foolishness.

It is good to know, enjoy, and understand these varieties (and, in truth, it's often easier to find and purchase them), but much of the excitement of wine is in discovering and uncovering wines that are unknown to most. Mencia, for example, or Plavac Mali, to name a couple of reds, and Pigato or Furmint, on the roster of less familiar whites, are often vinified into exceedingly delicious wines. But the selected varieties are unimportant. Choosing to spend a bit of time, study, and tasting to expand your life in wine is what counts.

So pick a grape variety and make it tell you all it knows. This can be a quick trip or a leisurely stroll, but either way, you'll soon be on the road to expertise, a very good place to be. *Na zdravje!*

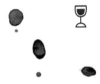

TWELVE
T W E L V E

TAKE NOTES

"To what end?" you ask. "I'd rather just drink and enjoy my wine, without all the bother of writing about it, too."

Well, well, and here I thought you were looking to love wine more. You can't just "use" this juice like it's coffee to keep your sleepy bones awake or cola to wash down your tuna salad at lunchtime and expect any progress on the quest to glimpse wine's inner sanctum. Consider the history, the complexity, the essential nature of our beloved beverage to humankind's ancient, and modern, existence. A gift to, and from, the gods. A symbol of fertility and regeneration. A stand-in for the blood of life, for the blood of death.

Taking notes isn't a precursor to a career in journalism, nor will it spoil the satisfaction of your evening's glass(es) of wine. In fact, it's not meant to be seen or read by anyone but you, or whomever you choose to share it with. It is not for general consumption: grammar is unimportant, complete sentences are a waste of time, and weird and personal notations are encouraged. It is, no more and no less, a tool of focus and memory and your advancement in the wonderful world of devotees.

Ask most folks if they like a wine and, if so, what they like about it, and responses are uniformly vague and uninteresting, incapable of transmitting any of the essential qualities or idiosyncrasies of the wine. Question a true lover of wine and the results are strikingly

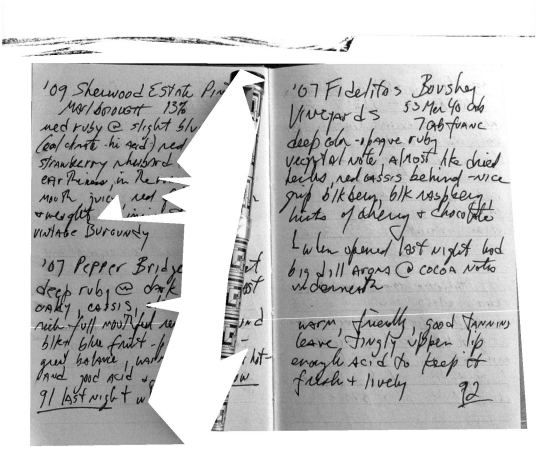

different: they can discuss specific aromas in the nose of a wine, the quality of its mouthfeel, its predominant flavors, levels of acidity and tannins, the length and intensity of its finish. In short, the latter can and will provide a profile of the wine that all wine drinkers can understand and appreciate.

Pay attention and jot some thoughts while you drink and you will soon be doing the same. That is the value of taking notes, to extend your own understanding and appreciation of what's in your glass. It is quite remarkable to define a wine with specificity—no more "it tastes good" or "it's really juicy." The act of taking notes forces you to focus, to pay closer attention, and to draw upon the best your brain has to offer. Yes, that's a pleasing smell, but what is it, exactly? The raspberry jam your granny used to make or the smell of fresh berries from the farmers' market? Is it raspberry or strawberry, rhubarb or currants? Is that tobacco you smell, and if so, is it fresh or dried, or more like the wonderful smell of the old cigar box that sat on the corner of your father's desk? Is the acid high or low or medium? Are the tannins rough, smooth, green and harsh, or fine and well-integrated?

These terms and qualities may trip you up at first. You have to focus, to pay attention—a wonderful step in learning to love wine more. Identify the smells and flavors you're enjoying; let them engulf your senses and they will reveal themselves. It may take some time, some moments of concentration, before you realize what that very familiar aroma or flavor is. Licorice, cinnamon, white pepper, pineapple, leather, lychee, melon, road tar, forest floor—all these and many other distinct aromas are present in wine, so don't be afraid to go there.

Recording your impressions of wine will not only encourage you to focus and fully enjoy what's sloshing back and forth in your glass, but it's also the key to remembering a wine and referring back to it in the future. If you have any kind of wine appetite, and obviously you do, otherwise you'd be reading *The Big Book of Designer Fishing Lures* about now, you'll eventually try so many wines that it becomes impossible to recall all the names and vintages. Note taking, by any method, will end the aggravation of forgetting the producer or name of that great bottle you'd like to find and buy again.

Smart phones and tablets (and who knows what's coming next?) make the entire procedure quick and painless. Back in the day, a wine lover had to write actual notes in an actual notebook, and if he or she wanted a visual reminder, the best options were to soak off the labels or be endowed with a photographic memory. Nowadays, with every phone and tablet armed with its own camera, recording a wine label has become a snap. And the apps available for taking notes and filing and sharing them are excellent. Find one you like and you'll be note taking like a pro.

There are two parts to good wine notation. The first concerns your physical, sensual impressions of a wine. Sensual in terms of stimulating your senses, as spelled out in the famous five S's of wine tasting: see, swirl, sniff, sip, and savor. So, to begin at the beginning, the first thing you do is see, or observe a wine. Look at and take note of the color, how dark or light it is—light ruby red or inky purple—and if the color shifts towards the rim of the glass—as wine ages, it develops a brown or amber edge—and finally, whether it appears bright and clean or shows some cloudiness or visible sediment.

Swirling is simply a technique to bring out a wine's aromas. The very thin layer of wine left coating the inside of a glass evaporates quickly and releases the wine's volatile compounds into the air and, hopefully, into your curious nostrils as well. And then … the sniff, the heart and soul of wine tasting. Close your eyes, shut out all those pesky distractions, and sniff deeply. Let the aromas inhabit you. Whatever it smells like to you is what it smells like to you. Make a note, multiple notes. Bright aromas of cherry and cedar to start, and after a while perhaps you discern dirt—the smell of earth, of soil—or rhubarb or the peel of an orange. Just write it down; no big deal.

Take a generous sip and let it rest in your mouth. Suck a draft of air over and across the wine. Then begin to work and chew it. It will break up and bubble and fill your mouth with sensations of weight and viscosity, acidity (that mouthwatering quality along the sides of your tongue) and tannins (dry, puckery lips, gums, or tongue) and perhaps sweetness or heat. It's here that a drinker assesses the harmony of a wine. Much of what makes a wine great depends on how well-balanced its various elements are. Extremes stick out and put either a rut or a ridge in what should be a seamless, sensual experience.

The alcohol level should be high enough to give the wine body and interest but not so high as to make it hot or harsh. Acid keeps a wine lively and makes it a good partner with food, but too much makes a wine tart and unpleasant while too little makes it soft and flabby. Tannins give a wine structure, something to "hang the fruit on," it might be said. Big prominent tannins curl your lips and dry your mouth. Thankfully, tannins soften and integrate with age, while wines with minimal tannin to begin with are often overrun with fruit and alcohol. No single attribute should stand out, though they often do. A wine may be excellent except ... it's just too soft and jammy or it's hot on the finish, too much alcohol. Whatever the reality, write it down, just a few quick notes to express the wine's character.

And here's the moment to focus on the flavors, understanding that "flavor" is a combination of the sweet, sour, salty, bitter, and umami impressions recorded by your mouth and tongue, and the smell sensations of specific substances—fruity, earthy, spicy, etc.— contributed by your retro-nasal epithelium, i.e., your "smeller" or your "sniffer" or whatever you want to call it.

Confirm whether or not the wine tastes like it smells. As you sip and contemplate, do you discern all the same fruit and wood and coconut and black pepper that you encountered in the sniff? Make note of the differences and the similarities. Develop a shorthand; note taking should be quick and capture a wine's essence. There's no need to scribble until your fingers are tired. Add a few words about the finish, the savor, last of our five S's. You might scratch out "short, falls off quickly" or "long, silky, focused, goes on forever."

You will notice a concentration on the absolutes—alcohol, acidity, and tannins—as these are the same for everyone, regardless of whether we all perceive them with the same clarity. Fifteen percent alcohol (on the high side) is 15%, no matter who is doing the tasting, whereas aroma and flavor associations vary from one person to the next. A friend may insist that a wine tastes of cherries and ground pepper while to me it's clearly strawberries and black tea. So who's right? No one; everyone. There are chemical, molecular structures behind these impressions, but as individuals we interpret information differently. You may associate a flavor compound with yellow apples while it reminds someone else of the almost-ripe Bartlett pears they used to filch from the orchard down the street when they were kids.

Hence, good notes done quickly highlight the absolutes of a wine and then you can dress them in personal analysis and perception. Remember, these are your notes. They reflect your sensations and sensitivities. They increase your focus and help implant a memory of the wine in your brain.

Once the bulk of the objective note taking has been completed, it's time to move to part two of the exercise. You know what the wine is, or at least how it should be described. Thin or full, hot or not, soft or tannic, long or short, violet or ruby, clear or cloudy, sweet or dry, you've particularized the measure of it. Should you sip the same wine next week, chances are good that you will describe it much as you already have. So, the question still to be answered is, do you like it?

Whether or not a particular concoction of alcohol and acid and tannins and flavonoids—that you have so carefully delineated—appeals to you is another consideration entirely. Accurately described though it may be, a wine can still be delicious to one taster and mediocre to another. As they say, "each to her own." You can summarize your response to a wine using any number of systems: many prefer to score it using the 100 point scale so easily relatable to grading in school. Others prefer a European twenty point system or the awarding of three, four or five stars. The more poetic among us may record

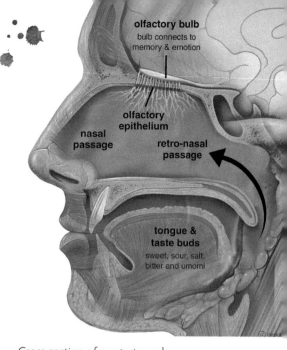

their impressions in language that would drive the critics to drink. "Like a citrus-tinged butterfly flitting through a garden of tropical fruit" or "it charges the palate like a bull in uniform with chocolate epaulettes and a peppery snort." Wow! Crazy stuff. But if images of flitting butterflies or rampaging bulls make sense to you, by all means, use them. Whatever approach you take is entirely dependent on your own preferences.

Cross-section of our taste and sniffer apparatus

The intent is not to be a professional critic. Your score or imagery speaks not to the objective assessment of how well-made a wine is or whether it should win awards but rather to your personal response and enjoyment. Would you buy it again; is this a wine you'd share with friends, or was it okay but hardly worth purchasing more of? The purpose here is to bring you closer to the essential elements of wine, to increase your familiarity and comfort level with wines of various sorts from various regions. Focus, scribble, assess, and remember.

Your notes will now comprise an objective evaluation of the wine, one that can easily be shared with friends and other habitués, and your personalized take on its appeal to you, something clearly worth remembering. With every focused thought, with every recorded impression, your wine acumen and perception are sharpened. And Bacchus thanks you for your efforts.

THIRTEEN

THIRTEEN

KNOW OLD WORLD VS. NEW WORLD

I T'S TIME TO DRINK SOME WINE, TO COMPARE AND CONTRAST, to distinguish one from another. Based on weather and soils and traditional tastes and methods of winemaking, Old World wines have a decidedly different personality from their New World counterparts. Distinguishing the two is, with certain exceptions, fairly easy and enables a greater understanding and appreciation of wines from different cultures and parts of the world.

The easiest approach is to let the wines teach you themselves. Of course, this means you will have to drink, and pay attention to what the wines tell you. I might suggest the following lineup: a New Zealand Sauvignon Blanc, probably from Marlborough, and a French Sancerre from the Loire Valley. Follow that pair with a white Burgundy, perhaps a simple Pouilly-Fuissé or, if you can, shell out a few more bucks for a Meursault, a Puligny-Montrachet, or a Chassagne-Montrachet. Compare any of these classic Old World white Burgundies with a reputable Chardonnay from California or Chile. Easy-to-find names to be considered, though there are many others, include Grgich Hills, Chateau St. Jean, Ferrari-Carano, Casa Lapostolle and Montes Alpha.

Now let's try some reds. A Barossa Valley Shiraz contrasted with a Crozes-Hermitage from the northern Rhone. Comparing these two areas of Syrah production, the former Australian and the latter French, will provide a clear picture of New World vs. Old. Next up, let's taste a Malbec from Argentina side-by-side with a Cahors (also Malbec) from southwest France. And if you would like still more clarification, pick up a Pinot Noir from a good appellation in California, the Santa Rita Hills or the Russian River Valley, to sip and assess against a French Burgundy—just about any well-made, decently priced *Bourgogne* will do. Or you could substitute a German Spätburgunder or an Italian Pinot Nero, all the same distinctive Pinot Noir grape to enjoy next to that California version you've picked up.

It's not required that you like any one of these better than its opposing partner—though you will—as the point of this exercise is to familiarize your palate with the differences between them, not to present or declare one as superior to the other. This is not a contest; it is rather an educational side-by-side. You'll realize that New World wines reflect, to a significant degree, warmer weather, fruit over minerality, and less variation from one year to the next. These are wines, much loved by many, that are decidedly fruit-forward, lower in tannins and acidity with a friendly, easy-to-drink savoriness to them.

Those of the Old World, the traditional heartland of modern wines, reflect the soils, the mineral quality in which these vines are grown. Every year is a new opportunity and some vintages are without question better than others. These wines value elegance and restraint; one needs a degree of curiosity and experience to appreciate the more reticent flavors and pronounced levels of tannin and acid that characterize them.

When a wine bursts onto your palate with gobs of fruit and little in the way of acid or tannins to hold it back, chances are good

that you're enjoying juice from Australia, New Zealand, South Africa, or the greater Western Hemisphere. If instead the minerality is distinct, the fruit restrained, and the entire gustatory experience more focused on balance, terroir, and exploiting, or displaying, vintage variation, it's likely that you're enjoying something Old World, something designed to accompany a meal rather than merely declare its deliciousness—or perhaps one should say voluptuousness.

Dirt, earth, soil, minerals, wood, leather, spice, and some fruit to enliven it—Old World. Fruit, juiciness, fruit, wood, fruit, coconut, and an overblown dose of alcohol on the finish—New World. That's not absolute—what is? There are plenty of Old World producers who have adopted the "international" or New World style, just as there are New World producers who value the complexity and control of the Old World.

Distinguishing them, however, gives you a certain insight into the character and priorities of the first major division in the world of wine. Many folks enjoy them both, each for their particular qualities. Others prefer one style over the other, as shown by what they most often drink, what makes up the bulk of their cellar, and what they serve to family, friends, and guests.

As with most things wine-related, there is no right or wrong. What you like is what counts, and knowing your way around the world of wine is certainly worth liking. Taste and learn, my valued friends. Skōl!

FOURTEEN
FOURTEEN

FOURTEEN

LEARN THE BASICS: VITICULTURE

THERE IS NO NEED TO ENROLL IN AGRICULTURAL SCHOOL, but understanding the basics of what can, does, and should or should not occur in the vineyard is a tremendous asset to understanding why a resulting wine is stunning, suspect, or merely so-so.

The viticulturist, aka winegrower or farmer, has plenty to keep him- or herself busy. Pruning, fertilizing, irrigating, canopy management, and pest and disease control are among their regular responsibilities. A good grape grower knows the soil, the weather, the drainage patterns, even the insect population of all a winery's vineyard sites, as well as the best trellising systems, plant density, and specific characteristics of the grape varieties being grown.

All of which revolve around the grape vine, a thick, woody liana that would prefer to wrap itself around a nearby tree and climb to the sun. And in fact, that's exactly how wild grape vines, *Vitis vinifera sylvestris*, do grow. Even the domesticated version, *Vitis vinifera vinifera*, is more than happy to take to the trees and reach for the sky, though it's also amenable to being trellised, pruned, and manipulated in service to its human caretakers. Much of the "trick" of grape growing is encouraging the plant to follow a course it wouldn't normally choose. The vine's innate objective is to grow and thrive, to cover new ground and engage in as much photosynthesis as possible; in other words, to eat, grow, and be happy. The grape growers' objective is to stymie much of that growth, to keep the vine in check and direct its energies not into extending its domain (sending shoots out here, there, and wherever possible) or increasing the number of its photosynthesizing leaves, but to create and care for its berries, the next generation, at the expense of its own immediate comfort.

If possible, a vine would prefer to grow ... by growing. And if conditions are favorable—fertile soil, sufficient water and sunshine—that's exactly what it will do. Like all vines, *Vitis vinifera* likes to sprout new leaves and tendrils, to overrun its current boundaries and conquer new territory. From the plant's perspective, this is right and just, the best-case scenario.

A wine grower's job is to corral these visions, to make life less comfortable, to the point where a vine sees little promise in its present locale and opts instead to channel its resources into the development of offspring, i.e., its seeds, hoping they will find a better situation and continue the blood, err, sap line somewhere else, someplace more akin to vinous paradise.

Kinda goofy, you're thinking, and how is that achieved, anyhow?

A handful of relevant concepts and understandings will put you in good stead. If it's been determined that vines produce superior grapes when they're "challenged" to find a better life, it should come as no surprise that soils and soil composition play a major role in determining the quality and wine-worthiness of the grapes of any particular vine. Rich fertile soils encourage a vine to pour more of its nutritional resources into producing leaves and shoots. There is less "floral concern" (as in *flora*) regarding the security of the lineage, the certainty of the next generation, i.e., the seeds, and therefore the grapes, when the environment is rich and welcoming. And so, for good wine grapes the best sites are decidedly bereft of nutrients. Preferred are poor soils that provide good physical support for the vine, are loose enough to drain efficiently, and have some mechanism to retain water at a greater depth, forcing the vines to deploy deeper roots and to allocate more of what they do have to the grapes instead of the leaves and shoots.

Wine growers adapt trellising systems most in tune with the terroir of their vineyards. For example, if a vineyard is located in warm or fertile or humid regions, the vines will often be trained in high, open systems. By raising the vines, leaves, and grape clusters

The basket vines of Santorini

higher off the ground and allowing a flow of air under and around the leaves and the grapes, it is possible to reduce the incidence of fungus or mildew and to keep the vines healthier. At the opposite end of the trellising spectrum are the basket-trained vines of the Greek islands, especially Santorini. Here the winds off the sea are strong and constant; the soil is poor, volcanic detritus. A young vine would have little chance of survival in such an inhospitable environment. But when trained into a circular basket shape, low to the ground and with the grape bunches protected inside the basket, these vines produce grapes capable of crisp, precise wines, bright, and filled with minerality and unmistakable presence.

Pruning leaves to open the canopy

Pruning, of course, is another technique. By strategically removing leaves, it's possible to open a canopy and allow more sunlight to reach the grapes. Shaded grapes tend to produce green vegetal wines. More light allows them to ripen and reach fuller maturity where their flavors are fruity and reflect the soil.

A problem referred to as over-cropping is also resolved by pruning. In essence, a vine produces a finite amount of food for itself, thanks to its broad, flat leaves, which convert sunlight, water, and CO_2 into sugars and other carbohydrates that in turn feed the leaves, the roots and stems, and the grapes. When too much of a plant's sugar production is directed back to its leaves, less is available to fuel the growth and development of its grapes. Through the strategic elimination of leaves (pruning) and thinning of the canopy, not only is more direct light made available to the grapes, but there is also less competition with leaves for the plant's food stores.

In essence, it's a matter of balance: with too few leaves catching sunlight, not enough photosynthesis takes place and the entire vine is undernourished; with too many leaves at work, there are more mouths—leaves and shoots and stems—to feed and the grapes are shortchanged.

Much the same can be said of water. Too much and the plant grows uncontrollably and the grapes' flavors are diluted; too little and the vines may even shut down and stop producing any sugars. So winegrowers aim for an appropriate level of water stress, enough to maintain photosynthesis and food production, but not so much that a vine turns into a Jack and the Beanstalk version of what it should be.

Grape growers refer to a vine's "vigor" and how important it is to keep this inherent tendency to grow in check. Good viticulture is not so much about limiting vigor, in the greater sense of the word, but about redirecting that vigor to the grapes themselves. And even then it's not uncommon to have too many grape bunches competing with one another for a plant's sugars and nutrients, in which case the savvy farmer prunes and discards bunches of grapes, as well as unwanted leaves and shoots. This so-called "green harvest," done before the grapes begin to change color, is another way of assuring that the remaining grapes are as good as they can possibly be.

You should by now have some sense of the winegrower's constant attention to and interaction with his or her vines. Still, there is more to be done. A vineyard site may be home to burrowing rodents or flocks of birds or insects carrying diseases that affect the plants. Various forms of mildew and other such fungal problems may also have to be dealt with. This might entail the use of pesticides or mixtures of copper sulfate and lime, for example, to protect the vines against disease or insect infestation. Most growers try to use as little of these substances as possible but a vineyard is a large open ecosystem that interacts with its environment in many ways.

In the neighborhood of 150 days after a vine shows its first signs of green growth in the spring (bud break), the grapes have matured

Measuring Brix levels with a refractometer

and are ready for harvest. Three aspects of a ripening grape that winegrowers keep a close eye on as harvest approaches are sugar, acid, and phenolic or physiological maturity. The amount of sugar in a grape determines the level of alcohol in the resulting wine. This is measured in degrees "Brix," with the final percentage of alcohol being slightly above half (about .60) the Brix reading. Hence a Brix measurement of 24° will produce a wine of about 14% alcohol.

As the winegrower measures this daily, waiting for the Brix to reach its desired level, he or she is also weighing the fact that increasing sugar means decreasing acidity. Wait too long to pick and the grapes will be high in sugar and potential alcohol but low in acid—not the recipe for a great wine. Acidity gives the wine life and brightness and allows it to accompany food with a decided *joie de vivre.* The theoretical "perfect" moment is when the two levels cross—not too much acid but still enough to give the wine verve, and sufficient sugar to make a wine strong but not hot or overly alcoholic.

A third consideration is physiological ripeness, a state where the tannins and other phenolic compounds that give a wine its color, flavor, and aromas are also fully mature. Depending on local conditions, this may or may not coincide with the optimal balance point of rising sugar and decreasing acidity. As you see, there is much to consider, including the weather forecast, so when a winegrower decides it's time to pick, everyone involved has to move quickly; even a day or two can make a difference in fruit quality.

Of course, with tens or hundreds of acres of vines, no single grape grower can accomplish all this without help. Whether they're driving tractors, pruning canopies, spreading fungicides, or picking the now ready-to-be-harvested grapes, there would be no wine without the skilled hands and untiring backs and knees of the farmworkers, many of them seasonal or migrant laborers, who perform these tasks.

Exactly who these people are varies from country to country and region to region. In Bordeaux one encounters Moroccans and north Africans; Germany and Austria favor workers from Poland and Romania; while vineyards in the United States depend largely on Mexican immigrants.

Making it all possible

Their story is as crucial to the existence of wine as good site selection or careful aging. As wine drinkers, we have many people to thank for our bounty and good fortune. Certainly a toast to the pruners and pickers is always in good taste. Here, here!

FIFTEEN

FIFTEEN

DECANT WITH PANACHE

WINE IS A MYSTERY, A BIG, COMPLEX, ALMOST UNKNOWABLE bundle of facts and fictions ranging from ancient history to leading-edge scientific development. Only a fool would dream that he or she can or should understand it all. If you need absolute certainty in life, clear-cut documentation of cause and effect, wine is most assuredly not the place to invest your time or energies. On the other hand, if shades of gray, hints of other truths, mysteries unsolvable give texture to your life, a sense of wonder and reality, you're probably right where you belong.

All of which brings us to the subject of decanting. Riddles, conundrums, and puzzles of organic chemistry abound in every bottle of wine. Certain additions and deletions do things for reasons unclear: too little oxygen, for example, may have a deleterious, though temporary, effect on wine; too much, for too long, is likewise a problem, though how much is too much and how long is too long is a predictive problem that modern science is unable to compute. Which leaves it, as with so many things vinous, up to the human senses of sight, smell, taste and touch to resolve.

Decanting, despite all the mumbo jumbo and when-do-you and when-don't-you and what kind of decanter should be used, is merely the addition of oxygen to wine. And why is that a good thing, you ask? Well … because it makes the wine taste better. Usually. What's more, decanting is fun, and instructive: it reveals how wine ages and evolves and gives you the chance to handle bottle and decanter with a bit of flourish.

Two situations call for decanting. The first is when preparing a younger, tight, muscular, tannic red to be enjoyed. A Barolo, perhaps, or a newly-released Brunello di Montalcino or left bank

Don't be afraid to splash and swirl when
decanting a young, tight red.

(Cabernet Sauvignon-based) Bordeaux. Something that curls your lips and pummels your palate. Anything that's a little tougher than you like to drink. And even if you're a tough guy, decanting one of these beauties will elicit subtleties and complexities and a harmony that you'd otherwise be unaware of.

In a way, decanting imitates the effects of aging. As a wine's multitude of phenols and esters interact with oxygen, tannins are softened and aromas enhanced. The wine takes on a more sensuous mouthfeel, losing its interest in clobbering your taste buds and instead coaxing them into an appreciation of the wine's better attributes. The nose opens and that complex interplay of fruit and spice and soil and wood replaces the closed, just-smells-like-wine aromas that you were struggling with earlier.

The technique is easily mastered. A young, brawny red is far from delicate. With a clean decanter in one hand and an open bottle in the other, just pour. Pour fast, pour hard, try not to spill. Some of us have even been known to shake the newly filled decanter, or pour a wine back and forth from one vessel to another, to mix in as much oxygen as possible. Depending on the wine—and you'll only learn this through trial and error—a half hour, an hour, two or three hours, or even the better part of a day, will greatly improve the wine's character and drinkability. And its deliciousness. Just to prove the point, leave a glass or so in the bottle when you fill the decanter, stick the cork back in, and when you finally welcome your guests to the table and fill their glasses from the decanter, pour a second, undecanted glass from the bottle and compare.

The decanted wine will exhibit a come-hither aspect, while the original will probably be closed, unyielding, and not interested in giving much to its imbiber. The same wine—one open and relaxed, filled with nuances and suggestion, the other tight, a shell drawn around it, uncommunicative. Such is the effect of exposing a hard but well-made red to the beneficence of oxygen and the patience of its drinker.

In theory, the more surface area exposed to air, the more efficacious its decanting. In other words, a wide-bottomed container that offers a larger surface to interact with oxygen encourages a more effective and successful decanting. So as to the question of a "right or wrong" type of decanter, one with a flared or horizontal orientation will do far more to aid the cause than a tall fancy piece of glassware that provides depth but little surface area to engage the O_2 in the surrounding atmosphere.

The second situation calling for a decanter is when you want to remove the sediment commonly found in certain types of wine. Thick-skinned reds (not to be confused with unfeeling communists), with an abundance of tannins and anthocyanins, the constituents that provide astringency and color, are particularly prone to developing sediment in the bottle. Many Shiraz from Australia, for example, even when young, are happy to coat the insides of their bottles with these harmless—though who enjoys a mouthful of coffee grounds?—grainy particles.

Wine science informs us that molecules of tannin and color combine, or polymerize, creating new and longer molecular chains that are simply too big to remain in suspension. Their size and weight cause them to drop out and fall either to the bottom of the bottle or, if a bottle is lying down, to the shoulder and sides of the bottle (much of the reason that aged reds are lighter in color and less tannic as well). Much as rain falls from the sky, sediment falls from the wine.

Older Cabernets, Ports, and reds that haven't been filtered—a conscious choice of the winemaker to minimize intervention that might reduce flavor—almost always "throw" some sediment. Even white wines come with their own version, looking like tiny chips of glass that are actually crystals of tartaric acid. Again, harmless, but no one needs a mouthful of hard gritty particles when trying to enjoy an otherwise good wine. Hence, decanting. Though in this circumstance the objective is eliminating sediment, not aerating the wine.

As might be imagined, the technique is slightly different. Pouring the wine fast and hard is exactly what should not be done in this case. Rough handling of the wine will only disturb, i.e., stir up, the sediment. If anything, a consciously gentle approach to the bottle and the procedure will keep the undesired sediment from swirling about and clouding the wine.

This decanting is best done with a source of light behind the bottle you're holding, be it a window, a lamp, an overhead light, a candle, or even the flashlight app on your cell phone. The purpose is to allow you to see the sediment sloshing along inside the bottle, trailing the pour, so that you can turn the bottle upright and end the process before all that sandy mess flows into the decanter.

In this situation, the wine is poured slowly and carefully so as to leave the sediment behind in the bottle. And then, when pouring from decanter to glass, one likewise pours with an easy hand to leave behind any sediment that may have made its way into the decanter.

This double filtration, as it were, gives a clean, drinkable glass, allowing us all to enjoy the winemaker's intent.

With very old wines, say twenty-plus years, it should be kept in mind that once decanted these wines should be enjoyed quickly. They're often fragile. They've lived in a reductive, i.e., oxygen-deprived, environment for many years. Too much air coming too quickly tends to knock them out. There is obviously a scientific explanation here, but the drinkers' reality is that such wines may "break up" within only fifteen or twenty minutes. Like the picture of Dorian Gray, these wines age to completion before our very palates. From stunning maturity to death in a matter of minutes. It's actually a rather singular experience and quite interesting, the takeaway being that you shouldn't decant that 1978 Bordeaux and set it aside for an hour while you enjoy an apéritif: there won't be much of value left to put in your glass.

Decanting is a little showy, a little fun. And completely called for in certain situations. So go ahead, buy yourself a piece of glassware, as plain or fancy as you like, that will hold 750 ml or more and make use of it. Not only is decanting visually enticing, but it creates an interactive relationship between drinker and wine. Rather cool. Check it out.

SIXTEEN
SIXTEEN

LEARN THE LINGO

THERE'S WINESPEAK, WHICH CAN LEAN DANGEROUSLY INTO the camp of affectation, and wine talk, which uses agreed-upon terms and vocabulary to discuss wine and all its wonderful permutations. Though one might wish otherwise, the two often overlap.

If you pick up some oenological terms and phraseology—though all serious commentary, questions, and observations should be accepted on their merits, it tells others that you care about wine, that you've made yourself available to wine and its influences. Speak a few words of Greek on your next trip to the Peloponnese and you'll be offered a richer experience by your very act of trying. In this regard, wine is no different.

No one learns an entire vocabulary in a single session, and there's little point in attempting to do so, but grabbing an occasional new, unknown, or alluring word as it flies by is highly recommended.

A couple of follow-up keystrokes on your computer or smartphone will bring one more facet of the world of wine into focus. Not to mention how welcome the feeling is of actually understanding what you're reading or what's being said around you. If you're an old-timer who still scribbles faster than you can text, the back pages of your tasting notebook (you do have a small booklet for tasting notes, don't you?) is the ideal spot for recording the words you would like to further explore.

Words specific to wine run the gamut from agricultural to vinicultural to the sensual. Many have clearly defined meanings and usage and help build the structure upon which wine discussion and knowledge is shared and passed on. Others, especially those used in tasting notes or to describe an individual wine, exist simply because we have so few words available with which to discuss the experience of taste or aroma. Somehow, smell and taste were shortchanged in our culture and assumed a fallback position of "tastes like ... " or "smells like ... ," comparing the actual sensation to something else.

For example, we have no vocabulary, no agreed-upon word or words, to describe the taste of a blueberry, or a carrot. Both are quite distinct, yet beyond the obvious good or bad, sweet or sour, how do we describe them? Sniff a bar of unscented soap and come up with a description that doesn't compare the smell to something else. It's practically impossible. Visually, we are able to describe objects or scenes in great detail; aurally, we can hear and reference tones and timbres and rhythms; tactile impressions are likewise easily relatable: soft, firm, gritty, smooth, slick, rough, hot, cold, and so on. But there's no way to describe to someone else the actual flavor of that blueberry using any generally under-stood or accepted vocabulary.

So we make comparisons. Or commandeer other words and apply them to specific attributes of wine. A wine tastes of licorice and black currants, or rhubarb and strawberries—always comparing its flavors and aromas to something else. Or it might be said that a wine is lean or fat, elegant or rustic. There's nothing wrong with this, that's just how it is. And it all works fine, as long as you understand the intent, the implied meaning of the stolen or comparative words.

It should, perhaps, be blamed on chemistry. After all, the senses in question, smell and taste, are entirely dependent on the play of specific chemicals upon either receptors in the mouth, commonly known as taste buds or those at the top of the sinus cavity, referred to as the olfactory epithelium. Substitute one molecule for another, even one atom for another, in whatever is being ingested and the tastes or aromas experienced can be completely different. In theory we could all become organic chemists and discuss the *4-(4-Hydroxyphenyl) butan-2-one* or the lack of *2-hydroxybutane-dioic acid* in a glass of wine, but it's so much easier to say the wine shows lovely notes of raspberry, though it's a bit flabby in the mouth.

And so, the words. The lingo, the phrases. Some precise, some explanatory, some descriptive. Not hard to learn and kinda fun to know. Ampelographer. Maceration. Over-cropped. Veraison. These were blanks for me at one time. Plant density. Loess. Sur lie. *Saignée*. These and other words I had to look up, many others, to be honest. But I did and I gradually came to a greater understanding and appreciation of the entire universe of wine, from grape varieties, to how and where they're grown, the various approaches to winemaking, and how to describe and discuss what I'm drinking.

On one hand, being a wine snob and tossing around terms and descriptors just to impress people makes you an ass, but on the other, absorbing the vocabulary and learning the language, at your own pace, allows you to share a marvelous experience with folks who love and enjoy wine as much as you do. It's surprising how quickly the brain responds, files, and categorizes what's just been collected, and offers it up at just the right time and place in a conversation or while digging into that new wine book. Our gray matter loves to be stimulated. Why deny it such a useful and much-deserved pleasure?

Think of what you are very good at, or what subjects you've had a long-term interest in. Sports? Baseball, football, hockey? Travel? Geography, photography, scenic locales? Music? Genres, tempo, instruments? Cooking? Foods, techniques, cuisines? Art? Color, perspective, history? Business? Stocks, marketing, balance sheets? The list could easily go on, but the point is that every area of interest has its own vocabulary, its own "zip lingo."

Knowing the terms commonly used is a major component of enjoying and excelling at anything. It opens the doors to a subject and reveals the inner workings. It's a connection to other enthusiasts; hell, it's your ticket to the best seats in the house. Is there a surfer out there who doesn't know what *frontside* or *kickflip* means? A rock climber who doesn't know what *scree* or *couloir* refers to? A gardener who's baffled by *deadheading* or *vermiculite*?

Definitely not. So hitch up your oenopants and start grabbing those new, unknown, not-completely-clear words you see, hear, and read in the course of sharing and savoring this wonderful beverage. Online, in a book, or in discussion with someone who is a little further down the vinous highway than yourself, find out what all those cool terms mean and how they're used. You'll be one step closer to excellence and enjoy one small smile every time you hear or see a word whose meaning you've just discovered.

Cheers to that!

SEVENTEEN
SEVENTEEN

DRINK OLDER VINTAGES

MOST WINE IS MEANT TO BE ENJOYED ALMOST IMMEDIATELY (within a year or two of the vintage date for whites and two or three for the reds; in other words, shortly after release). Who doesn't like that fresh, fruity glass of young Torrontés or Pinot Bianco? Or the lovely, lively taste of Barbera or Beaujolais? And while few reds will actually go bad if you hold them for a bit longer—though not many will greatly improve—light-bodied whites may well show signs of aging relatively soon.

Young wines of any color have a ... hmmm, youthfulness to them. They are bright and eager to please. They lap your face like a puppy, make you happy, and demand little thought or attention in return. Just drink me, they say, and I'll reward you with a glass of deliciousness to go along with that tasty meal you're about to enjoy. A lighthearted, useful attitude and one that informs much of our selection process for picking out, from among the many options, "tonight's" wine.

But as friendly and tasty as these not-meant-for-aging wines can be, their older, more venerable cousins bring elements to the table, or glass, proving that patience is indeed a virtue. These senior members of the grape-juice clan may have outgrown the high jinks of youth—the lip-smacking acid or the withering tannins or the jumble of fruit flavors and sheer power—but they've picked up a whole new bag of tricks along the way.

Instead of running around your taste buds and trying to impress with their pure exuberance and lust for life—not a bad thing, by the way—they've acquired skills and nuances and organoleptic wisdom, tricks of the taste-stimulating trade that make their youth seem absolutely misspent.

At first it's a bit disconcerting, the contrast of old vs. new. But once you've moved beyond the fresh fruitiness of a young, well-made wine and experienced the complexities, the singularity, the crème brulée-ish flavors of a mature red, you'll think differently about the benefits of older vintages. Impatient drinkers declare that life is short or question how much better an older wine can be. The answer is "much better"—more complex, more enticing, more complete. Just let those good wines in your possession rest and relax and be overlooked for a few years. Ignore and forget them. Buy other bottles to fulfill the daily requirements.

It's easy enough to acquire three or four bottles of what impresses you, what shows a healthy dose of tannins and acid, markers for a wine with age-ability. Drink one or two and let the others fade into your "collection" of wines, to be reconsidered at some point in the future.

Old wines have class. They're delighted to introduce you to the tertiary flavors of aging, to the vanilla and tobacco and cigar box flavors and aromas of a wine that has reached maturity. A beautiful young Bordeaux, all power and sinewy insistence, is no match for the same wine wearing the cloak of maturity. What's more, there is great

fun in opening older bottles that should be over the hill—always a possibility—yet encountering a wine of marvelous flavor and complexity. Popping corks on older bottles—but do it carefully, as those corks have a tendency to dry out and become brittle—is like being a hustler tossing dice against the vagaries of time, in cask and in bottle.

When it works out as desired, it's a marvelous experience. Think red or white wine with a dash of smoke and vanilla, softer tannins, a suppler body, an enticing, seductive complexity that's hard to resist. The best are profound, the rest merely exciting. Yet there's nothing that tastes quite like a well-aged wine. And the nose! Holy cow, vintner man, my little sniffer can barely keep up. Store a living, evolving bottle of juice in the dark, without oxygen, for a dozen or so years and then let it get a big breath of fresh air and all kinds of amazing things can and do happen.

Older bottles don't all travel the same path, even those from the same vintage and the same producer. What's called "bottle variation" is a very real phenomenon. Storing your wines in a cool, dark location, like a dedicated wine cellar or cooler, if possible, will increase the odds, but there's never a guarantee on the final outcome. That's just part of the mystery of wine. Many a wine geek has opened a thirty-year-old bottle with the fill level below the shoulder—a very bad sign—and been stunned by the magnificence of the wine inside. Just as we've all opened a bottle of ten or fifteen years, in pristine condition that's been cellared since release, only to find that Father Time has already come and gone, or perhaps it was the Grim Reaper.

But no matter, because those gems of old far outshine the few that fail to complete the journey. It's quite remarkable to sip an aged glass of wine and consider the world as it was when the grapes were grown and picked and put into the fermenter, to reflect on the events in history or in your own family that were happening as this wine was being born. The stories some of those bottles can tell—and will, if you let them.

And so, let us raise a glass and give a shout. To the Maine!

EIGHTEEN
EIGHTEEN

LEARN THE BASICS: VINICULTURE

THE CONVERSION OF GRAPES TO WINE IS A REMARKABLY simple process. Grape juice is laden with sugars, primarily glucose and fructose. Fermentation is the action of yeast—a strange and ever-hungry single-celled organism—that ingests sugar and excretes (a terrible image, but how else to explain it?) alcohol and carbon dioxide. The CO_2 bubbles away during fermentation and then you and I drink the alcohol.

What's unique is that these yeast conveniently live in colonies on the outside surface of the grapes, so it takes no more than a break in the grape skin to allow yeast to enter and begin chowing down on all the lovely, sugar-laden juice inside. In other words, if one were to merely toss a few bunches of grapes into a container, breaking some of the skins in the process, fermentation would begin spontaneously, such that within a few days, depending on the weather and temperature, one would have wine. Not barrel-aged, not filtered of its particulate matter, but wine nonetheless. Such was the genesis of human identification, utilization, and understanding of wine. And things didn't change much for many thousands of years.

Oh, sure, people chiseled out depressions in stone slabs to contain the grapes, which they now crushed by stomping on them, and further refined the containers and—once pottery was developed—jars or jugs, into which the juice was transferred to ferment. They learned to plant vines in rows and to give them something, a trellis, a tree, a forked stick in the ground, to grow on; they came to understand that wine exposed to air spoiled quickly, and so the concept of "stoppers" came into being, the first being perhaps a twist of grasses stuck in the neck of a jar; and they learned to "fine" wine by dropping an egg or some other natural product into a wine to remove unwanted "things" floating around or suspended in their treasured libation. To sum up, people were, as long as eight or nine thousand years ago, making wine with the same basic techniques, though in a more rudimentary fashion, that we utilize today.

Not much besides tweaks to the existing process came into being for thousands of years. Winemaking was a fully mature—as in well-understood and widely practiced—endeavor before the advent of writing. It's part of the human experience and has lubricated religious belief and ceremonies and social respite and interaction since time immemorial. It wasn't until Louis Pasteur uncloaked the science of fermentation (all those yeast gobbling sugars, etc.) in the 1850s, and the advent of stainless steel tanks a bit later, that winemaking evolved into the well-understood, scientific undertaking it is today.

Though in fact, due to vagaries of weather and fruit quality, of tannins and acids, of yeasts and nutrients, winemaking is as much art as science. Each vintage presents the winemaker with a slew of options and challenges, choices between doing this or that, and all have an effect on the final product.

In modern wineries the newly picked grapes are first subject to inspection, usually by way of riding a conveyor belt while quick hands pluck out the bad grapes, twigs, or anything else not welcome in the finished product (think dead bugs and loose feathers).

From there the bunches usually have an appointment in the crusher/destemmer, a modern convenience that replaces the foot stomping of old, breaking the grape skins and simultaneously separating berries from stems. Some winemakers want the stems left in their fermenting "must," but most prefer to avoid the extra dose of tannins that stems impart to a wine. Though it sounds complicated, a crusher/destemmer is a rather simple piece of equipment, essentially a bin with an auger at the bottom that does all the work.

At this point, the grapes for white wines are sent to the press where they're squeezed to extract their juice, which is then poured off and transferred to a fermenter while the remaining skins and seeds—after being pressed perhaps a second or third time—are discarded or added to the vineyard's compost pile.

Practiced hands removing the MOG (matter other than grapes)

Punching down to extract added color, flavor, and tannins

With dark-skinned grapes intended for the production of red wine, the must—a slurry of juice, pulp, skins, and seeds—is pumped into a fermenter without first being pressed. As this mixture ferments, color is leeched from the skins into the otherwise clear juice, and the skins, seeds, and stems together contribute the tannins required to give structure and texture to the red wine. Carbon dioxide bubbling to the surface during fermentation carries with it the mass of skins and other solid matter, which form a "cap" floating atop the nascent wine.

Since the objective is to infuse the wine with the anthocyanins (the main source of color), the tannins, the flavonoids, and the esters that give wine its taste and aromas, all of which are found in the grape skins and seeds, it's necessary to break apart that cap of goodies and push it back down into the wine so proper maceration can occur. This can be done by "punching down" using a stick with a flat disc on the end or by "pumping over," which is simply pumping juice from lower in the fermenter onto the surface of the cap, causing it to break apart and sink into the liquid. The more often this is done—two or three times a day is not uncommon—the darker and more structured the wine will be.

Red wine is often (usually?) fermented in open top containers, whether of oak, stainless steel, concrete, or plastic. The presence of CO_2 caught up in the tiny nooks and crannies of the cap creates a protective barrier—assisted by the antioxidant qualities of the grape skins' color molecules—against excess oxygen or airborne bacteria. The open top also helps by releasing heat, stimulating the yeast, and allowing easy access to the cap for punching down.

Once fermentation is complete, the new wine is racked off (transferred to another vessel) and the remaining solid matter is pressed to extract a further dose of color and tannins. Depending on the winemaker's objective, this "press wine" may or may not be added back to the wine itself.

Red wine usually undergoes an additional fermentation to reduce its acidity and smooth out its texture and mouthfeel. This "malolactic fermentation" is driven by bacteria rather than yeast and converts a portion of the rather harsh malic acid to softer, rounder lactic acid. From there the wine is most often moved into barriques or other styles or sizes of oak containers for aging.

Meanwhile, since the juice of white grapes is racked off its crushed skins, stems, and seeds before fermentation, it's more vulnerable to contamination and is typically dosed with sulfur to fend off the incursion of microbes or oxygenation. It is then transferred to either wooden casks or closed stainless steel fermenters (which permit more precise temperature control while the yeast are heating things up, devouring the sugars and transforming them into alcohol

Cleaning—the job that's never done

and CO_2). Cooler fermentation temperatures also preserve more of the primary fruit character especially important to white wine.

Once fermentation is complete, white wines may also undergo malolactic fermentation, although many whites are defined by their acidity and changing its nature is not always the right move. In the case of crisp, bright whites from many of the world's significant wine regions, vintners often choose not to employ malolactic. Typically, rich full-bodied Chardonnays will undergo MF, while taut, lively Albariños will not.

Another process that most white wines benefit from is the removal of tartaric acid, in crystalline form, from the wine. "Cold stabilization," lowering the temperature of the wine close to freezing, causes the tartaric acid to precipitate out and be left behind when the wine is racked off, either to spend time in oak or to be bottled and shipped to market.

While this is a broad-brush summary of the winemaking process, it provides a fairly complete picture of the winemaker's focus for two or three months—of eighteen- or twenty-hour days, in most cases—immediately following harvest. The physical work of sorting, crushing, pressing, fermenting, punching down, racking off, stabilizing, etc., involves long stretches and hundreds of decisions that will affect the final character and quality of the wine. Lifting, lowering, turning, pumping, dragging, pushing, rolling, shifting, shoving, and cleaning. Oy, the cleaning! Days in rubber boots and wet shirts, hosing, rinsing, scrubbing, washing, and doing it all over again, and again, ad infinitum.

All while testing, monitoring, sensing, and choosing. Should we pump over once more today, or do we have enough tannin and color at this point? Do the yeast have sufficient nutrients to last through fermentation? Is the temperature too low, or too high? How much sugar is left in the must and how much do we want to be left? Is the acidity where it should be? Are we emphasizing fruit or the earthy, minerally aspect of the wine?

And so it goes, with decisions about exhausted workers, broken tractors, miscalibrated lab equipment, burned-out pumps, leaky seals, and what and how to feed the crew every day to keep them happy and productive thrown in, just to be sure the winemaker has no rest whatsoever. Ah, but they're junkies. They love it. And look forward to it every year. Just as we look forward to sampling and slurping each new vintage of our favorite wines and wineries. Quite a symbiosis, wouldn't you say? A toast, to all the world's winemakers, cellar rats, and harvest hands!

NINETEEN

NINETEEN

SALMON AND CHÂTEAUNEUF-DU-PAPE: A BIG, BROODING RED AND A HUNK OF FISH?

A BIT ODD, I'LL ADMIT, ON FIRST CONSIDERATION. SURE, we've all heard the contrarian cry of red wine with fish, but who imagined that it was far less radical than we'd previously thought? Introduced to me by Lulu O., a tough, tiny whirlwind of Gallic blood arrived in central Massachusetts by way of small-town Ontario and before that the outskirts of Paris, a journey of some four generations. She and her husband, the wine-loving doctor and Chevalier du Tastevin, who've wallowed in the pleasures of France far more than I, who take joy in food and wine and know them both, sat me down and without ado served.

A glistening slab of meaty, poached pale-orange dressed with a delightfully simple white sauce, thick with body and texture, studded with shallots and tomatoes and cream. "You'll like this," I was told, as the doctor poured.

I'd imagined a big white, a Burgundy perhaps, or possibly a lighter red. He is, after all, a Burgundian at heart, a devotee of the Pinot Noir. But he also pays attention; he learns and experiments, and when the somms of Lyon pour a hefty, hearty Châteauneuf-du-Pape to accompany that lovely serving of salmon, the canny Frenchman takes note. So Châteauneuf-du-Pape it is.

How is one *not* to love the bright red fruit, the cinnamon and licorice and flecks of tobacco, the weight and texture, the swirl of plums and berries, regardless of the fare? But how beautifully the fatty fish and the unctuous cream, shallots, and tomatoes married to one of southern France's great bold red wines. And though a surprise, it was a magnificent pairing, leading one to realize that elements of so many dishes sing aloud when presented with the virtues of so very many wines.

There are synergies afoot, complexities and layerings of flavor. Every culture has its age-old pairings of food and wine that on the surface make little sense but have, nonetheless, survived the generations and become a cornerstone of local gastronomy. To wit: Sauternes and foie gras; Lambrusco and *salumi*; Rioja and seafood paella; Negroamaro with pasta and chickpeas (*ciceri e tria*), and anchovies thrown in for good measure.

Of course, there are some food and wine combinations that do not work. Period. Both the food and the drink are worse for the attempt. These are quickly apparent, though may differ based on your specific palate. In any case, it's the experimentation that will make you smile; that will add confidence and dimension to your basic love of post-fermentation grape juice. Be it hot dogs and Italian whites, salmon and Châteauneuf-du-Pape, or any other duo of deliciousness that you might stumble across, never underestimate the possibilities of very good food with very good wine.

It's food, after all, that in many ways defines a wine. The back and forth of textures, acid, weight, and flavors give substance and reality to Bacchus's creation. There is an inherent, almost primal, harmony between the two. In many cultures wine is food, an integral part of the meal. And a meal without wine is either unthinkable or sorely diminished. In such cultures one seldom drinks wine without food; together they form a gesture of thanks given for the earth's bounty. Whether vegetables from the garden, wine from the vineyard, or meat from the pasture, the produce of the land is best enjoyed shared with friends and family.

To the gods, to the farmers, to the Frenchmen ... bottoms up!

20

TWENTY
TWENTY

REVIEW SOME RECENT HISTORY

D^{O YOU KNOW THAT BEFORE THE CIVIL WAR, THE} Cincinnati area was the Napa Valley of its day? Or that the number of wineries in Washington state grew from 163 in 2000 to 850-plus as of 2015? Or that one of history's greatest wine frauds was perpetrated by an Indonesian immigrant living illegally in California who sold tens of millions of dollars of fake wine to the world's wealthiest and, supposedly, most astute collectors?

The first question hints at a longer, more robust American connection with wine than we may have thought, a connection, in fact, that extends back to our earliest European colonists. And if any wine region, anywhere in the world, experiences the kind of explosive growth that Washington state has seen, it's a clear sign that something worth knowing about is underway. Finally, who doesn't love a great scandal, a train wreck of social contract taking place before our very eyes?

The full history of wine in the United States is fascinating. Richer and more complex than we generally acknowledge. Most wine buffs are aware of Thomas Jefferson's love of wine and his early attempts to plant vineyards, but how many know of the English crown's desire that Jamestown and Plymouth would produce wine on a commercial scale, in part to improve its trade balance with France? Or that California, with a winemaking tradition dating back to the Spanish missions, would be set on its modern course by a young aristocrat who escaped (barely) the Russian revolution? Or that 80% of California wines were sweet as recently as the 1930s? There are so many stories, compelling narratives of overcoming the odds, of prescient thinking, of thievery run rampant.

There is much to learn, fascinating stories of the twists and turns in the enological landscape, not just of the U.S. but of the entire world, that have occurred in the past two hundred and fifty years or so that no one who cares about wine should deny themselves the enjoyment of exploring and learning more about.

In all aspects of wine, things have morphed and evolved, been lost and found, treasured and trashed. Whether discussing Bordeaux or Champagne, Chianti or Port, the Yarra Valley or the sub-regions of Mendoza or the emergence of Georgia, grape varieties and bottle types and farming practices and trade routes and yeast strains and barrel sizes and sulfur usage and fermentation practices and sugar and alcohol levels and so many other particulars have shifted and adapted, and all of it together has brought us to where we are today. And that's just the technical changes; the social and political vicissitudes are even more compelling.

Some of the topics worth exploring include:

- A twenty-seven-year-old widow who shook up production methods and built one of the world's great Champagne houses

- The re-emergence of Hungarian Tokaji to the world stage of dessert wines after the fall of the Soviet Union

- The impact of the 1848 California Gold Rush on that state's evolution as a wine region

- The official Paris luncheon between French President Sarkozy and Iraqi Prime Minister Nouri al-Maliki that was canceled because the Iraqis objected to wine being served or even placed on the tables

- Repeated instances of producers and wholesalers in Burgundy blending in cheap wine from elsewhere to build their inventory of pricey bottles in weak vintages

- How in the 1960s David Lett and a handful of Pinot Noir lovers took a chance in the Willamette Valley and created Oregon's spectacular wine industry

- Two thousand-year-old almost-lost varietals like Greco di Tufo, Falanghina and Fiano, rescued from extinction only in the past few decades and now available for your drinking pleasure

- Dramatic and ongoing changes in U.S. shipping laws that make it possible, or not, to receive wine at home, depending on where you live

By dipping minds and palates into the swirling pool of recent wine lore, we enhance our understanding of what's actually in our lovely stemmed glasses, of how it came to be, and why it's better or worse than we may have expected. We get a grip on the continuum, a box seat at the play of Vines & Wines. Even better, we get a glimpse of the people, the heroes and the frauds, the sirens and schmucks, the folks and facilitators, the inhabitants, the citizens, the vintners, the brokers and merchants and everyone else who informs the current oenoscape.

Anyone can drink, but knowing the back story lends a certain deliciousness to the endeavor (and who doesn't love that?). Wine is a summation of human experience and as such touches on everything

Wine fraud gets bigger, bolder and more creative.

from agriculture to chemistry to physiology to economics to war and peace and, most definitely, crime and punishment. Did you know that during World War II, French vignerons hid much of their wine in secret underground caves to keep the Nazis from looting it? Or that just before Prohibition, little Stone Hill Winery in Missouri was producing more than five million bottles of wine every year and winning awards across Europe?

The stories, the human side of wine, are fascinating. Just trying this wine or that, perhaps based on reviews or recommendations, provides a very tasty experience, but it's like watching a sporting event and not knowing any of the players. Does she usually make that very difficult shot or was it a foolish attempt? Is there added emotion because we've learned that the coach has just lost a close family member? Is the new player on the field fighting to keep his job because of off-field antics? These are the nuances that give flavor and immediacy to the game, that enrich our viewing pleasure.

You fill in the back story of wine by reading—books, blogs, magazines—and listening, by traveling and experiencing, and by keeping your eyes and ears open. The information is all there, available to you whenever you're ready for it.

A few books you might enjoy in that regard include:

- *The Billionaire's Vinegar: The Mystery of the World's Most Expensive Bottle of Wine,* by Benjamin Wallace

- *Judgment of Paris,* by George M. Taber

- *Wine and War: The French, the Nazis, and the Battle for France's Greatest Treasure,* by Donald and Petie Kladstrup

- *The House of Mondavi: The Rise and Fall of an American Wine Dynasty,* by Julia Flynn Siler

- *Napa: The Story of an American Eden,* by James Conaway

- *Wine Wars: The Curse of the Blue Nun, the Miracle of Two Buck Chuck, and the Revenge of the Terroirists,* by Mike Veseth

- *The Vineyard at the End of the World: Maverick Winemakers and the Rebirth of Malbec,* by Ian Mount

- *The Widow Clicquot: The Story of a Champagne Empire and the Woman Who Ruled It,* by Tilar J. Mazzeo

- *The Botanist and the Vintner: How Wine Was Saved for the World,* by Christy Campbell

- *In Vino Duplicitas: The Rise and Fall of a Wine Forger Extraordinaire,* by Peter Hellman

- *Thirsty Dragon: China's Lust for Bordeaux and the Threat to the World's Best Wines,* by Suzanne Mustacich

- *Shadows in the Vineyard: The True Story of the Plot to Poison the World's Greatest Wine,* by Maximillian Potter

A nice case of wine books, an even dozen, though there are dozens more. Pick up one or two. Start reading. Enjoy the stories of wine, of winemakers, of dreamers and movers and shakers. There is so much humanity swimming about in our oceans of vino. Learn the technical stuff, too, if you have a mind to. It's fascinating, of unending interest. Of course, it must all be undertaken with a bottle of something very good at your elbow and a glass of the same in hand. Salud. To context.

TWENTY-ONE
T W E N T Y - O N E

VISIT A WINERY

THE TITLE OF THIS CHAPTER MAY SEEM OBVIOUS, BUT MANY wine enthusiasts have never been inside a winery, never inhaled that funky, enticing aroma of crushed grapes or had someone point out the cooling jacket on a fermenter and explain how it works. Look, many of us don't live in California or Bordeaux or Tuscany. It's not like there's a winery just down the road that we can pop into whenever we want ... or is there?

Actually, if you're among those who have yet to step across the crush pad, to meander among the old oak vats and the concrete eggs and the stainless steel fermentation tanks, luck may be on your side. Chances are quite good that almost anywhere you live, there's a winery much closer to you than would have been the case ten or fifteen years ago. The incredible upswing in new and rejuvenated wine regions—think Priorat or Virginia or the Colchagua Valley— whether thanks to an improved economic outlook—Mendoza, Tokaj and the Dalmatian coast come to mind—or the silver lining in the clouds of global warming—the Okanagan Valley or even southern England—means that it's very likely there *is* a winery just down the road. Might be time for some popping in.

Whether you live in Sussex or southern Ontario, in Colorado, Columbus, or the Florida panhandle, you're not far from a winery, or wineries. In the U.S. wineries now operate in all fifty states. An afternoon drive may be all it takes to enjoy a quick lesson, with expert instruction, on the care and feeding of a working winery. If you're an old hand at this, think back to the excitement of your first few visits: seeing the bins of just-picked grapes, maybe watching the fermenter bubble or the floors being hosed down, the heady aromas of grapes and alcohol.

Or perhaps you've visited midwinter, when the atmosphere is relaxed and the winemaker him- or herself shows you around. You'll quickly get a new sense of size and scale and a clearer picture of

Hard at work in St. Emilion

how it all happens. While tasting room visits are fun, be sure you take advantage of the winery tour. What they're making—be it a fine Cabernet or strawberry wine—isn't as important as *how* they do it. Look at the equipment, the tanks and bins and racks and pumps and hoses and barrels, and envision the process from start to finish. Ask questions. Get answers. Whether you're in Missouri or Long Island (or Germany or France or the South Island of New Zealand), the overall methods and equipment are essentially the same.

In some regions it may be common practice to use concrete fermenters, while other areas or wineries favor oak or stainless steel fermentation tanks. Some winemakers age their wares in barriques, oak barrels holding 59 U.S. gallons, though others prefer 150-gallon puncheons or 1500-gallon oak vats. But it's still fermentation and it's still aging regardless of the specifics.

You may show up in time to observe the bottling process or to watch winery workers chip crystals of tartaric acid from inside the tanks used for cold stabilization or see the pomace being shoveled from a fermenter after the wine has been racked off and transferred to a different vessel.

And in the cave or chai or barrel room, depending on where the winery is located, you'll have the chance to cast your gaze over vintages' worth of finished wine awaiting its time in rows of barrels and tanks of varying shapes and sizes.

It's the perfect time to clear up any misunderstandings you may have, so if the particulars of malolactic fermentation or the process for inoculating the must with a strain of commercial yeast are a bit vague, let Bacchus move you to the front of the group that you might

Welcome to Klinker Brick Winery

pose your questions directly to the winemaker. As much as winemakers want you to understand the overall process, it's the geeky questions that get them jazzed. This is their bailiwick; winemakers love to discuss the specifics, the minutiae, the technicalities of their chosen vocation. It's in such details that their knowledge and their individuality as vintners presents itself.

A single caveat: for the purposes of both education and loving wine more, large commercial wineries are best avoided. Presses that you can see in operation and hoses being attached and unattached and fining and filtering that you can observe give a much clearer picture of the progression from freshly picked grapes to finished juice. Large wineries, unfortunately, resemble nothing so much as refineries; in fact, should you be from an area beset with oil or chemical plants, you'd feel like you had never left home.

There's something decidedly unromantic about a multi-acre agglomeration of Bunyanesque holding tanks connected by a network of overhead pipes and the occasional metal building housing one or more important functions of the overall operation. Certainly you can take it on someone's word that must is being transferred and yeast is being added and pump-overs are internal and automatic. Though I see neither grapes nor spills of wine nor evidence of living, organic matter, I do see a pipe and I'm told the wine is flowing through it right now from one computer-controlled tank to another. Oh, be still my beating heart.

Of course, wine (some wine) has to be produced in huge quantities. Otherwise, how could our growing thirst for it be satisfied?

Much of this mass-produced juice is quite drinkable, some of it very good indeed, though the factory (no other word fits so exactly) where it's produced allows no visual, visceral connection to the end product. And as the purpose of a winery visit is to absorb, to see and smell and understand the conversion of grapes to wine as has been practiced for some thousands of years, the closer to the process you can put yourself, the more rewarding your visit will be.

You'll have more fun, and feel more of a connection, with a winemaker who crafts his or her wines by hand. By taste and look and instinct and experience. All winemakers use lab tests, and you can find a computer in most every winery, but that's a long way from total automation. Keep in mind that mass production is a function of demand and market size and modern transportation. Its products range from why bother to excellent. It sells because it is sold. But artisanal, handcrafted products are the result of passion. Of caring and time and patience. They sell because they're good, very good, and sometimes sublime.

Find a little winery with a few acres of grapes and a team led by a winemaker who's in love with what he or she does. Ask how they do it. Let them show you around. Take it all in. Taste and smell and look and listen and pull it around you like a cloak of anointed human endeavor. And I bet a little of that love will rub off on you, too. Happy hunting.

DO A TASTING OF DESSERT WINES

A H, THE SWEET STUFF. SOME WINE LOVERS CAN'T GET enough; others hardly touch it. In fact, it's a remarkable category. Depending on the style, dessert wine may be enjoyed by itself, with cheese or nuts, or as an accompaniment to a luscious meal-ending sweet. Though the technical aspects of creating dessert wines are surely interesting, it's another of its sensual characteristics that I find even more compelling.

And that's the color—the hue, the intensity, the sheer beauty of a lineup of sweet wines that excites the visual senses. Pour a young Barsac (flagrant yellow) next to a Sauternes (yellow with golden-orange highlights), followed by an Eiswein (a glowing sunset), a New World Muscat (pure orange), a Rutherglen sticky (amber/orange), a Tawny Port (like the name says), a Ruby Port (pure ruby red), a Malmsey Madeira (red/orange brown) and a PX Sherry (dark, raisiny). What a chorus line of legs and lights.

The high sugar content makes these wines more viscous than regular table wines, and they reward us first with their gorgeous light-capturing, eye-candyish appeal. It really is possible to stare into, or through, your glass of dessert wine almost forever, to contemplate your life and your loves and losses.

These remarkable extremists of the wine world, thanks to their excess sugar and acid, can age for far longer than we. With each passing

Sauternes all in a row – such a lovely lineup

decade, they get darker and richer in color, and less sweet and more captivating—more complex—at the same time.

However, now that we've acknowledged their shimmering shades of golden yellow through rich ambers and ruby reds, their light-bending ability to delight the eye and their complete comfort in being laid down for year after year, let us consider their genesis. Sweet wines, and dessert wine in particular, share a singular characteristic, that being elevated levels of sugar. As one might imagine, there are but two paths to excessive residual sugar in a finished wine. The first is to kill or incapacitate all those sugar-gobbling yeast before their appetites are sated and all the sugar ingested. The second is to increase the amount of sugar in the grapes being used, to the point where even those hungry yeast fail in their quest to join the clean plate club.

Yeast, it turns out, are not that dissimilar to the rest of living organisms. Too much heat kills them, too much cold stuns them. And about that alcohol—remember that yeast ingest sugar and excrete alcohol and CO_2. In fact, the chemists write it this way:

$$C_6H_{12}O_6 + Zymase \rightarrow 2\ C_2H_5OH + 2\ CO_2$$

where a molecule of sucrose, in the presence of zymase (an enzyme found in our friends the yeast) yields two molecules of ethyl alcohol and two molecules of carbon dioxide. All well and good until the alcohol level hits 15%, at which point the yeast themselves start dying.

In essence, a winemaker can stop fermentation when the remaining sugar reaches its desired level (say, 10%) by adding neutral grape spirits that boost the overall alcohol content above 15%. This is the standard production method for Port, Madeira, and Vin Doux Naturels, a French category that includes Muscat de Beaume-de-Venise and Banyuls. (Never heard of these? Put them on the shopping list for this amazing tasting you're assembling.)

The second approach, that of increasing the sugar content of the grapes themselves, is accomplished via a fascinating variety of grape growing, harvesting, and handling methods. The first and simplest of these is to let the grapes go unpicked beyond the normal harvest date. In most cases, this occurs when the grapes' acid and sugar levels are in balance. By leaving the grapes to hang beyond this point, the sugar content continues to increase. Depending on the duration of this extended hang time, the grapes begin drying out, concentrating their sugars even more. Some grapes are left for an extra week or two, others until they're practically raisins.

Where climactic conditions encourage damp, foggy mornings and hot, dry afternoons, late-harvest grapes may be further affected by a nasty-looking fungus known to wine lovers as "noble rot." Properly referred to as *Botrytis cinerea*, spores of this beneficent form of mold puncture the ripe grape skins and release water, leaving behind a more concentrated mass of sugar and acid.

Wines made from these desiccated berries have a highly-prized and quite distinctive flavor of honey, with a slightly bitter finish. Since *Botrytis* doesn't attack all the grapes in a cluster at the same time, each infected berry must be individually picked. Crews often make three or four passes through the vineyard to complete their task. Should afternoons stay damp and humid like the mornings, a variant fungus, i.e., gray rot (noble's evil twin) will ruin the entire crop. But when the rot's just right, the wine is divine.

Many of the world's great dessert wines, including Tokaji (Hungarian, from Furmint grapes), Sauternes (French, primarily Sémillon), and Trockenbeerenauslesen (German, hello Riesling), owe their existence to this unpleasant-appearing companion.

Next is the approach of letting picked grapes dry to concentrate the sugars. This *passito* method is used for the production of Amarone della Valpolicella as well as various dessert wines. By letting grapes dry, or "raisinate," we again benefit from concentrated sugars and the unctuous wines that result. Grape clusters are laid out on bamboo or straw mats, stacked in open-air "houses," and allowed to shrivel under the influence of local winds and air currents.

This is an ancient technique, with references to 800 B.C. and earlier by the Greek poet Hesiod. Multiple wines, delicious all, are so produced. In ancient times, because the higher sugar and acidity of these wines

Grapes for Vin Santo drying on the racks

ensured a longer shelf life than wines that were fermented dry, these sweet, almost voluptuous wines were highly prized. Vin Santo, Recioto della Valpolicella, and Passito di Pantelleria all fall into this category.

The final technique for boosting sugar in wine grapes is to leave them unpicked into the depths of winter. When frozen, water (as ice) is easily separated from the sugars, acids and other solid materials in the grapes. Vinification is of a concentrated must and produces a gorgeous, silky sweet wine renowned for its enticing mouthfeel and remarkable complexity. The most magnificent ice wines, or Eisweins, hail from Austria, Germany, and Canada.

Of course, the extra work of late picking, adding spirits, or laying grapes out on drying racks translates into higher costs. But typically such wines are sold in smaller bottles—375 ml and 500 ml—at quite reasonable prices. These are intense wines; the average pour is half or less of a "normal" serving of regular table wine. Purchasing half bottles is an excellent way to assemble a diverse lineup—for all your sweetest friends.

Put together a tasting of five or six of these beauties and you will be encircled by adventurous wine lovers drawn to your table, amazed at the beauty of your offerings, delighted by the magnificence of this delectable selection. As will you. Hats off and sweets to the sweet.

TWENTY-THREE

DISCOVER AND EXPLORE SHERRY

I T'S SURPRISING HOW FEW PEOPLE, WINE LOVERS INCLUDED, know the ins and outs of Sherry. Many think it's a single wine, or not a wine, or a dessert wine, when in fact it's an entire multifaceted family of wines, ranging from bone dry to unctuously sweet. An anglicized derivation of *Xeres* (the modern Jerez), Sherry is named for the region of its origin, a triangular territory in the far southwestern corner of Spain, defined by the towns of Jerez de la Frontera, Sanlúcar de Barrameda and El Puerto de Santa Maria.

Okay, great. So the wine has a somewhat strange etymology and comes from a hot, remote corner of Spain. Tell me again why I should care?

Fair enough; point taken. While there is no shortage of tasty, interesting, and obscure wines to be discovered, Sherry really does offer something worthy of your consideration. As stated, it's not just a wine—it's a category of wines, as varied and historically significant as

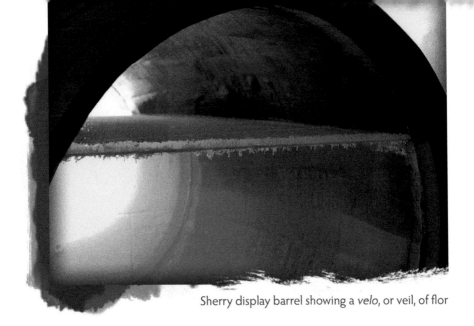

Sherry display barrel showing a *velo*, or veil, of flor

any other and, as it dates from the days of the Phoenicians, far older than most. There is much to Sherry, but three aspects in particular sing to the wine geek a sweet siren song.

First, among its most distinctive elements is a process completely counter to the production of anything you'd choose to put in your mouth. The most elegant of Sherries (aka Finos and Manzanillas) are aged for years under a blanket of fungus that floats atop its surface. This fuzzy gray-white mat, known as *flor*, is a layer of yeast that sprouts almost immediately after the wine completes fermentation. The finest, most delicate of these newly-made wines are fortified with a mix of neutral grape spirits and older Sherry to a strength of 15% to 15.5% abv (alcohol by volume), a level of alcohol adored by the flor. This process of biological aging protects the wine from oxygen and strips it of glycerin and volatile acidity while at the same time reducing its alcoholic content. The result is an exceedingly dry, light-bodied wine unlike any other.

Second, Sherry's unique process of fractional aging, utilizing a solera system, is a mathematician's delight. Set aside a large well-used, neutral barrel and fill it about five-sixths full of new wine. After it has evolved for a year or more, fill another barrel with another new wine, and so on until you have many levels of barrels containing successively younger vintages of wine. To bottle, a portion of the oldest barrel is drawn off, which is then replenished by an equal amount from the next-oldest barrel, which in turn is replenished by the same amount drawn from the third oldest barrel, etc., until all the barrels have been topped off with wine from the barrel immediately above them.

After a period of years, the older barrels especially contain a mixture of many vintages. There are soleras forty, sixty, even a hundred or more years old, still maintained and still having wine drawn from their oldest casks for bottling. As Sherries are bottled NV, or non-vintage, determining an average or accurate age is unnecessary—and best left to those with a facility for numbers and arithmetic calculation. What those of us get who love to drink the stuff, however, is remarkable consistency, and a freshness and vibrancy that simply can't be found in any equally old, traditionally aged wine.

Number three on the list of Sherry's most compelling aspects is its price. Low. Inexpensive. *Barato*. Excellent Sherries abound at ridiculous prices. Ignoring cheap cooking Sherry, as one most certainly should, it's still a breeze to find outstanding examples for less than twenty dollars a bottle. And since Sherry is often available in half bottles, your total layout for a great tasting of six or eight samples can be less than the cost of a single bottle of very good Bordeaux.

And that's just the half of it!

Remember, the most delicate of the newly fermented wines, those destined to become Finos or Manzanillas (Manzanilla is simply a Fino that is aged in the coastal town of Sanlúcar de Barrameda, where, it is felt, the sea breezes impart an additional freshness and salinity to the wine), are fortified to 15% to 15.5% abv to encourage the growth of flor. Those that don't make the cut, that are too robust, too full and rounded, are instead fortified to a level of 17% to 18% abv, which kills any emerging flor and prevents it from developing again.

This wine, put into its own solera with barrels also filled to five-sixths full but minus the "protective" layer of flor, will age oxidatively and become Olorosos, the fullest and richest of the dry Sherries.

Whether Fino or Oloroso, dry Sherries are greatly influenced by the Palomino grapes from which they are made and the *albariza*, or white, chalky soils, in which the grapes are grown. Rather than displaying much in the fruit department, the Palomino grapes tend

In a solera, Sherry is bottled from the bottom, or oldest, barrels.

to express the calcareous, or limestone, nature of the albariza, lending the wine mineral and saline notes.

So while Finos are light and complex, with sea spray and almonds, oyster shell, and perhaps even yeasty or citrusy notes (a perfect accompaniment to nuts and olives and fried seafood), Olorosos are all that and more: more broad-shouldered, richer in body and mouthfeel, tasting of walnuts, clove, dried figs and black tea, a local favorite to serve with heavier tapas, red meat, and game.

In some instances, the *velo de flor* dies off by itself. Maybe a cask in the solera wasn't refreshed with younger wine often enough and the flor failed from a lack of nutrients; maybe alcohol was added purposely to develop the intermediate Amontillado style. Amontillados are highly regarded (ask Edgar Allan Poe). After their beginning as a Fino or Manzanilla aging biologically under flor, they continue aging, but now in the oxidative style (i.e., without the oxygen-blocking layer of flor) of an Oloroso.

Most wines are protected from oxygen. Barrels are topped off on a regular basis to bar excess oxygen from influencing the wine; sulfur is added throughout the winemaking process in large part due to its antioxidant effects. And yet here is a wine that's deliberately

A beautiful lineup of Sherries

exposed to oxygen, where the deeper color and rich, nutty, and almost broth-like flavors are considered desirable. Other wines that celebrate oxygenation and flaunt their umami qualities include old-style white Riojas, Vin Jaune from the Jura region of France and, of course, Madeira, not only oxidized but cooked as well!

Between Amontillados and Olorosos lie the Palo Cortados, which likewise begin their vinous sojourn under flor. Unlike Amontillados, however, Palo Cortados show a fuller, more robust body, closer in weight and brawniness to a pure Oloroso. They typically have less finesse than a Fino/Manzanilla turned Amontillado, but are leaner and more precise, thanks to their (limited) time under flor, than a typical Oloroso.

Not to be outdone are the sweeter styles of Sherry. Vinified primarily from dried Pedro Ximénez grapes, often with a bit of Muscatel included, PX wines are ultra-sweet, rich, viscous, even treacly when young. With age they settle down a bit, losing their intense dried-fruit sweetness and becoming somewhat lighter in body. PX develops complex flavors of coffee, chocolate, raisins, and licorice as their stay in the solera is extended. Another popular version of sweet Sherry results from blending PX with Amontillado or Oloroso, proportions varying from somewhat to very sweet. These

Cream Sherries, as they are known, have a long history and are still quite popular, and the best are delicious, harmonious wines.

As the lover of wine quickly discovers, there is much to consider when exploring Sherry. To give a quick and easy summary, in order of body and delicacy:

- Fino and Manzanilla – the lightest styles, biologically aged, emphasizing saline, yeasty and almond notes.

- Amontillado – a Fino-bodied wine that loses its flor, usually after four to eight years, and completes aging oxidatively, still lithe but with a nutty, umami quality.

- Palo Cortado – a fuller-bodied wine that loses its flor rather early, shows more oxidative notes, briny, cinnamon, hints of dried fruit.

- Oloroso – richest of the dry styles, no flor influence, robust, nutty, broth-like, walnuts and tea.

- Cream Sherry – a variety of blends: pale, medium or *amoroso*. Olorosos or even Amontillados blended with a bit of PX. Many are commercial, but the best are lovely and elegant.

- PX – Pedro Ximénez, rich, intensely sweet. Older examples are very complex, very dark, yet lighter in body and bursting with coffee, spices, dates and raisins.

A great Sherry tasting may offer one or two versions of every style. It may compare Finos with Olorosos, a contrast of biological vs. oxidative aging. It may be a teaching tool to discern the subtler differences between Amontillados and Palo Cortados. It might even include a PX or Cream Sherry in a lineup of other dessert wines. There are no rules, only the pleasure of exploration.

Some winos fall down with joy when they first taste a quality Sherry; others find that it's not their thing. Both biological and oxidative aging imbue flavors not usually found in regular table wines. You may love them all; you may enjoy Finos but find that you have little taste for Olorosos. It matters not. As always, we can only be true to our own palates. Perhaps the real beauty of Sherry, in all its iterations, is to show us another way, another set of flavors, one that lies outside our norm and expands our oenological horizon. And for that alone, you've gotta love 'em.

TWENTY-FOUR
TWENTY-FOUR

CREATE A COUNTRY CHART

ARE YOU A LIST MAKER? DO YOU ENJOY KEEPING TRACK OF things, writing and recording what you've done or would like to do? If so, this chapter will certainly speak to, and appreciate, your organizational inner self.

While it's amazing how many countries produce wine—remember, there has to be a climate conducive to grape growing *somewhere* within a country's borders—it can be even more surprising to keep tabs on how many wines of various nations you have tried. A simple chart is the easiest way to track your own vinous adventures. Just list the countries whose wines you have had or would like to sample. Sort of a grapey birdwatcher's list.

Countries can be arranged by production, in which case you would have France, Italy, Spain, the United States, Argentina, Australia, South Africa, China, Chile, Germany, Russia, Portugal, Romania, Greece, New Zealand, Hungary, Brazil, Moldova, Austria, and Ukraine in the first twenty spots. (These may appear in a slightly different order depending on which organization's statistics are used and from what year.) Clearly, it's easier for most of us to find a wine from Austria than one from Romania, but that's part of the fun. Or you might arrange a chart with less emphasis on production volume and instead make use of a geographic orientation.

In that case, under your heading for "Europe" would be France, Italy, Spain, Portugal, England, Croatia, Slovenia, Germany, Hungary, Austria, Bulgaria, Romania, Switzerland, Macedonia, and Greece (assuming we don't consider Russia, Turkey, et al to be part of Europe but rather of central Asia). "South America" would list Argentina, Chile, Peru, Uruguay, and Brazil. And so on, until you had the entire world's major wine-producing countries on your chart.

	South America	
1	Argentina	√
2	Chile	√
3	Uruguay	
4	Peru	
5	Brazil	

While it's very cool to check off Brazil, Uruguay, Slovenia, and Macedonia, to collect wines and tastes from locations around the globe, this still leaves a lot of room for a deeper dive into the wonderful world of wine. The next step in geeky appreciation is to expand your charts to include the signature regions and varieties of the countries you have listed. After all, having enjoyed a bottle of wine from France or Italy, or even Austria or Greece, hardly gives one an idea or indication of the wonderful array of wines those countries produce. One bottle may be a start, but it's a little like sitting in a new car without actually having driven it. Instead of settling for such a limited experience, why not rethink (and re-drink) the chart to gain a more complete experience of the flavors and aromas each nation has available to entice its wine-loving admirers?

ITALY		
Region:	**Piemonte**	
red	Barolo	
red	Barbaresco	
red	Barbera	
red	Dolcetto	
white	Gavi	
white	Arneis	
Region:	**Alto Adige**	
red	Schiava	
red	Lagrein	
red	Pinot Nero	

If you've gotten this far, there's reason to believe a true aficionado dwells within, in which case a chart that deals in greater depth, one country at a time, might better serve your interests.

How detailed you wish to get is completely up to you and the level of your curiosity about exploring the wines of any particular nation. We all have the resources, be they Internet- or book-based, to search first for the major wine regions of a country and second for the major wines produced in each of those regions.

Looking at Italy, which is probably the most wine-heavily populated country of all, a search of the "major" wine regions generates Piemonte, Trentino-Alto Adige, Friuli-Venezia Giulia, Veneto, Tuscany, Apulia, Campania, Sardinia, and Sicily. Of course, Italy is one giant vineyard, or at least one gigantic array of vineyards, so leaving *anywhere* out will exclude important, well-known wines, though you will still have such iconic wines as Barolo, Barbera, Barbaresco, Pinot Grigio, Pinot Bianco, Friulano, Valpolicella, Amarone, Soave, Prosecco, Chianti, Brunello di Montalcino, Primitivo, Taurasi, Greco di Tufo, Fiano di Avellino, Cannonau, Vermentino, Negroamaro and Nero d'Avola, among others, to help you shape an image of what Italy has to offer. Far from complete, to be sure, but an excellent start nonetheless.

Other countries may have fewer regions to list or have fewer signature wines per region, but following this fairly simple procedure will expose you to more of the world's great wines in a straightforward, systematic manner than almost any other approach.

One continent, one country, one region at a time. It's a gorgeous way to tour the world and taste your way through vineyards old and new, high and low, warm and cool, inland or nestled by the sea. Remember, wine speaks to you only when you drink it—and you have to love that.

TWENTY-FIVE
TWENTY-FIVE

COMPARE 'BUBBLIES'

BUBBLIES, AKA SPARKLING OR CHAMPERS OR FIZZ, ARE fun—and celebratory, romantic, even historic. Beautiful, too. Beautiful to look at. Whether launching ships and boats, welcoming the new year, cheering a great success, or wishing a newly joined couple bounteous love and good fortune, we turn to these delightful wines for situations joyful and uplifting.

We all know Champagne, the most famous of this category; and most of us know that Champagne refers specifically, and exclusively, to the sparkling wines of the Champagne region of France. If you have purchased Champagne, either in a restaurant or a wine shop, you also know that it tends to be expensive. Yet bubblies are produced worldwide by a variety of processes using a variety of grape types. The glory of these wines lies in the dazzling skill of the vignerons who make the best of them, and the smile-inducing economy (i.e., low prices) of much of the rest.

The *méthode traditionnelle,* sometimes called the *méthode champenoise,* is a magic act of winemaking. It begins with the fermentation of grapes into a "regular" still wine, albeit one with high acid, low alcohol and neutral flavors. Some of the grapes, depending on the region, are likely to be red- or black-skinned varieties and must be handled quickly and cleanly to avoid leaching color into the intended "white" wine. At this point, most table (i.e., non-sparkling) wines are near completion, waiting only to be filtered and aged, if desired by the winemaker, and bottled. Champagne, however, and other sparkling wines are just getting underway.

Champagne houses, or brands or labels, each have a distinct style that their reputation is built on. It may be more or less lean or full, with a bit of fruit, or instead quite minerally, perhaps showing toast or brioche or crème brulée, light and delicate or hale and robust. The challenge, the skill, is to re-create that style on a consistent basis, year in and year out.

Enter the blenders. An individual or a group, members of the family, the winemaker with or without assistants, or assistance, but all with incredible palates and wine memories. The job now is to blend wine from multiple vineyard parcels, often from multiple years, into a cuvée that will undergo a second, induced fermentation in the bottle, be left to age for years under pressure, on its lees, will have some small amount of sugar added and be left to age again, and will finally be bottled and released. So the simple task is to create a blend that years later, after multiple manipulations, will taste just as the "house style" is expected to.

What a crazy, French, traditional, marvelous thing to do!

No one could argue that these aren't the best blenders in the world. The capability of their palates is ... wow, impressive, prodigious, covetable. It's not unusual to blend twenty-five, thirty, fifty, or more wines into a single NV (non-vintage) release. And if you drink Krug or Bollinger or Taittinger or Veuve Clicquot or Moët & Chandon or any one of a dozen other Champagnes on anything approaching a regular basis, you know just how impressive, and accurate, these folks are in envisioning and maintaining the house style.

After the blend is created—*assemblage*, they call the process— it's bottled along with a pinch of fresh yeast and a dose of sugar and crown-capped like a bottle of beer. The combination of yeast and sugar, of course, means fermentation, and more alcohol and more CO_2, which is exactly what's desired. Having no escape, the carbon dioxide is forced into solution in the wine, its characteristic buildup of internal pressure dependent on how long this second fermentation continues until the sugar is consumed and the yeast die off.

At which point the lees, the dead yeast, succumb to gravity and drift to the bottom of the bottle to begin their enzymatic self-destruction, or autolysis, which adds a creamy mouthfeel and flavors of bread and biscuit to the wine. Champagne must age thus, *sur lie*,

Crown-capped Champagne aging in a riddling rack

Frozen yeast ready for disgorgement

for a minimum of twelve months, though many producers routinely age even their non-vintage bottlings for three, four, or more years, giving their product much of its wonderful character. Cava, Crémant, and other sparkling wines also made in the *méthode traditionnelle* are usually aged for shorter periods of time.

As the wine approaches the end of this phase of its evolution, the bottles are placed in a riddling rack and gradually turned bottoms-up, with the dead yeast cells slowly drifting to the neck of the bottle. In time, all this sediment congregates behind the bottle cap. Since no one wants a mouthful of sediment or a bottle of cloudy wine, this accumulation of dead yeast is removed by plunging the bottle neck into a solution of freezing brine to solidify the plug of yeast. The cap is removed and the pressure of the CO_2 neatly pops the frozen bullet of yeast out, a technique known as disgorgement. To correct for the reduction in volume, a small measure of wine with a variable amount of sugar, the *dosage*, is used to the fill the bottle before it is corked and topped with the familiar wire cage, properly known as the *muselet*. Within a few weeks, or a bit longer, the Champagne is released and ready to be enjoyed.

It all sounds rather complicated, because it is. The storage, handling, and multiple steps involved in its creation make any sparkling wine produced in the traditional method a remarkable accomplishment. It took many years, from the mid-1600s to the mid-1800s, with contributions from insightful doers and thinkers like the famed monk Dom Pérignon, scientists Christopher Merret and Jean-Antoine Chaptal, pharmacist André François, and the winemaker Barbe-Nicole (Madame) Clicquot to fully understand and develop the techniques that allow us to enjoy such an upbeat, celebratory beverage.

The immense popularity of Champagne, especially in the capital cities of London, Paris, and St. Petersburg, spawned a host of imitators, a trend that continues to this day. The two Old World bubblies having the most in common with Champagne are Crémant and Cava. Crémants are made in France, using the same *méthode traditionnelle* production techniques, but hail from outside the region of Champagne. Depending on their locale, they may also contain different grape varieties. Cavas are a product of Spain, also made in the *méthode traditionnelle*, but generally composed of the Spanish varieties Macabeo, Parellada, and Xarel·lo. These are both delicious alternatives to Champagne, sometimes with a bit less complexity due to a shorter aging regimen, but at typically less than half the price, they're much easier on the wallet.

Other Champagne-like sparklers include Franciacorta, from Italy, a very classy wine also made in the *méthode traditionnelle*, there known as *metodo classico*, and the higher-quality sparkling wines of the United States and, increasingly, Canada and England. These are likewise products of the traditional method, though they often contain grapes not permitted in Champagne and may have different aging requirements.

Less regulated, less complex, and less expensive methods of sparkling wine production include the Charmat and transfer methods. Both involve the wines spending time in a pressurized tank, as opposed to remaining in their original bottles, either during or after the second fermentation. Such wines tend to be less intense than Champagne, with coarser bubbles and a creamy rather than fizzy mousse. Yet, for many, they are as intriguing and satisfying as their more pricey *méthode traditionnelle* cousins.

Of late, the wine world has seen a resurgence of rustic, unfiltered sparklers made in the *méthode ancestrale*, wherein a wine is bottled before its primary fermentation is complete, and often topped with only a crown cap. These so-called pét-nats, or *pétillant-naturels* (natural sparklers), are simple, low alcohol quaffs that have become quite popular.

In many countries sparkling wine production may include some or all of these approaches; a good look at the label should tell you which type you're considering. In addition to the regions named, look for tasty bubblies from South Africa (Cap Classique), New Zealand, Hungary, Portugal, and Chile. Italy offers numerous options besides Franciacorta, such as Prosecco and Asti Spumante, while Australia is home to sparkling Shiraz, a bold, refreshing red that can be just right if you're looking for the flavors of dark cherries, berries, and hints of chocolate.

Yet, it's hard to tell which of these lively options most suits your own palate without trying them side by side. And since prices range from less than $10 a bottle to well over $100, there is also the price/value ratio to consider. So line them up, call some friends, and give these various bubblies a try. (This might be the perfect opportunity to put your *sabrage* skills from Chapter One to the test, at least to kick off the tasting!) There are folks who swoon over Prosecco but find Champagne too intense. Italian Brachetto may be your bag, or perhaps an Espumante from Portugal. Hungary and Chile—whodathunkit—are other favorites, and Gran Reserva Cava is so Champagne-like it's almost indistinguishable.

Some sparkling wines are creamier than others; some show pronounced aromas and flavors of bread and yeast while others are more fruit-focused; this one may have tiny bubbles that go on forever while that one has an initial burst of big, lively bubbles that dissipate quickly. All these factors and others affect the mouthfeel, the texture, the aromas, the flavor, the finish, and the enjoyment that each individual derives from the wine. Remember, no two palates are alike. One of the things we love about wine is its diversity of styles and flavors, and our nearly unlimited options to find the wine that we most enjoy, that speaks to us and tickles our fancy.

Let's end this chapter with a quick rundown of sparkling wine styles and what they mean vis-à-vis what's in the bottle. While most bubblies are a blend of varieties, you will note some labeled **Blanc de Blancs**, meaning they are made entirely from white grapes, or **Blanc** *de Noirs*, meaning they contain only red or black grapes. *Rosés*, often showcasing lovely fruit notes, have acquired their color either by resting on red grape skins or by simply having a bit of red wine added to the mix.

As for the dry vs. sweetness scale, at one extreme are the wines labeled *Brut Natural* or perhaps *Brut Zero*, bone-dry versions that get no secondary dose of sugar, followed by *Extra Brut* and then *Brut*, both of which are dry and crisp. For a noticeable touch of sweetness, the categories of *Extra Dry*, or *Extra Sec*, and *Dry*, or *Sec,* belie their nomenclature and are actually on the sweeter side. For a very sweet bubbly, look to a *Demi-Sec*, and moving into dessert territory, the sweetest of all will be labeled *Doux* or *Dulce*.

Now that you're armed with some background and at least a partial vision of the huge spectrum of sparkling wines produced around the world, go out and corral a few. The tasting will be a delight, and you're going to love finding a new best "friend" for your future celebrations. Cheers!

26

TWENTY-SIX
TWENTY-SIX

DOWNLOAD A WINE 'FLASHCARD' APP

WHEN THE BRIGHTEST MINDS IN THE WINE WORLD study for advanced certifications, hoping to earn honorifics such as Master Sommelier or Master of Wine, they are pushed to expand both the breadth and the depth of their wine knowledge to almost unknowable extremes. They do this, certainly, for career advancement, and for self-validation or an oversize ego boost, as do all of us who study to be tested and then recognized and rewarded for our achievement.

And yet, beyond the desire to stand out within a small group of like-minded experts, they do it for love. For love of the subject—i.e., for their love of wine. They do it to feed and nurture their fascination with ... a beverage, with a sensual experience, with a history as complex and compelling as any history, and longer than most. They do it because the vineyards of southern Spain, originally planted by

Phoenicians when the Assyrians were at the height of power in the Middle East, when camels were first being domesticated for human use and the Olmec civilization was just emerging in Central America, are still producing grapes for winemaking. Because the delicate, finicky Pinot Noir grape, which until recently only produced top-quality wine in a small region of central France, is now a lauded varietal in more than a dozen wine regions around the world. Because winemakers and grape growers now use satellite images to identify the health and characteristics of their vineyards, row by row, and soon, with the advent of drones, vine by vine! In other words, how could one *not* be fascinated by this you-can-never-learn-it-all-but-you-can-sure-love-drinking-it-along-the-way subject?

And what tool, what very simple learning aid, do these thirsty minds use to fix the facts more firmly in their vinous brains? Why, it's flashcards. By the hundreds if not thousands. Most written by hand from another source: a book or a lecture, points of science, geography, service, appreciation, and so forth. Things as straightforward as "Merlot is the offspring of Cabernet Franc and what other grape variety?" and "Name three nutrients most important for a healthy grapevine," and "Where is the Coquimbo wine region?" These questions are undoubtedly on the "geeky" side (the answers are Magdeleine Noire des Charentes; nitrogen, phosphorus, and potassium; and Chile), but the point remains that flashcards are a quick and effective means of enhancing your growing wine smarts.

What's more, thanks to technology, if we choose not to, we have no need to handwrite dozens of individual cards emphasizing the gaps in our knowledge or the aspects of wine we'd like to brush up on or learn more about. Nor must we keep track of all those cards and slips of paper with questions on one side and answers on the other.

Instead, we can just open the app, on our phone or tablet or whatever we're looking at apps on these days, and pick up another tidbit or two of wine information. Learning has never been easier or more convenient. Waiting for a friend, for a class to begin, for the doctor or dentist or your ride to show up? It's impressive how much you can absorb in bits and snippets; good stuff that can assist your decision making when standing in front of the Vranac shelf in the local wine shop and your compadres have no idea what you're looking at.

Wine apps can be lousy or terrific, so read the reviews before downloading. Many are little more than tasting notes or compilations of regions or grape varieties, but even these can be useful. My current favorite, though new ones appear often, is the free SWE Wine and Spirits Quiz. Test-prep and study-guide apps are most likely to feature a flashcard-type platform; they're just right for killing a few minutes here and there.

Apps and learning modules, most of which are free or quite inexpensive, are listed under a diversity of categories, not just "Food and Drink." Look also at "Education," "Entertainment," "Games," "Lifestyle," and "Reference" as additional categories to check.

If you're online there are even more options for flashcards and other quick and easy learning guides. Just search the term "wine flashcards" and you'll get an array of cards and study guides well worth the time to explore. The card sets and practice exams at the Society of Wine Educators, for example, are first-rate and well worth the price. Of course, writing them yourself does reinforce memory (just ask any medical student, another group of learners addicted to the efficacy of flashcards), and many online sites will allow you to create your own set of cards.

Whether using a prearranged set or one you've cobbled together yourself, it's almost a guarantee that spending a few minutes here and there "playing" with your phone or computer will increase your understanding and appreciation of wine. And who doesn't love that? *Eskerriska!*

TWENTY-SEVEN
TWENTY-SEVEN

ENVISION TERROIR

THERE IS AN EXHILARATION ONE FEELS STANDING IN A vineyard, a soft breeze sweeping down the hillside and through the rows, watching the canopies move and sway as the wind sets them in motion, the sun warming the back of your neck, the smell of the broken earth rising from beneath your feet. There may be a view of water, of a river or an ocean beyond the next line of hills. In so many vineyards, the orderly regiments of vines that march up and down hugging the contours of the terrain provide a striking contrast to the drifting clouds and the mountains and the broken ridges of rock giving a sense of "place" to this field of grapes.

It seems everyone in the wine world has some relationship with the concept of terroir. Whether you think that soil type, wind, rain, sunshine, duration of daylight, air temperature, elevation, aspect, trellising, water stress, and so forth have a noticeable influence on a resulting wine or that terroir's impact on a finished wine is poppycock, the real determinants being grape variety and winemaking decisions, including approaches to aging and storage, may well depend on where you live and what you drink.

For those weaned on wines blended from grapes of multiple, geographically disconnected vineyards (think certain wines of California or southeast Australia, in particular), the winemaker is all-powerful and proof that terroir is a vacuous construct. Others, however, be they Napa Cabernet lovers or champions of Burgundy's Pinot Noirs, will declare to their dying day that site matters, that place is everything.

It's true that some wines suggest *somewhere*, while others, no matter how good, give no suggestion of place. While the best of both are delicious, envisioning the wine you're drinking in ways that extend beyond the glass adds a delectable, if not quite definable, element to the experience. I like to consider wine not only in terms of its place of origin but also of its place in time.

There is a tradition in wine, less important now than in the past, of buying and laying down a special wine at the birth of a child. When such a wine is opened and shared with the now-grown offspring, eighteen or twenty-one or some years later, it holds a special place, a temporal reminder, if you will, of the time as well as the place of its genesis. Imagining the vineyard, as well as the contemporaneous events surrounding both the plot of land and the date of vintage, fixes a wine within a magnificent geo/historical context. It makes it more interesting, man. More real, and more relevant.

Let us consider an extreme example. Château Musar, 1990. A winery dedicated to reestablishing the ancient Lebanese (i.e., Phoenician) winemaking industry and its former renown for elegant, perfumed wines. One man, the late Serge Hochar, its driving force. Vineyards on the west side of the Bekaa Valley. Waning days of the Lebanese civil war. Harvest among a sporadic hail of mortar shells. Picture this: an ancient land, vineyards marching away from your vantage point on the upper slopes of the valley, the sights and smells

Vineyard of the Languedoc region of southern France

of war, of exploded cordite all around you. Workers feverishly picking and loading trucks with the precious grapes. Everyone in for the forty-five mile ride back to the winery. But there's no way through. War and militias and renewed shooting. Detour. And another detour. The long way around, up and over the hills. Finally, some hundred and fifty sketchy miles later, arrival. Let the crush begin.

Now, try drinking a wine like that without a deeper appreciation and respect for all that went into creating it. Envisioning both the physical reality and the concurrent events imbues such a wine, or any wine, with qualities that are hard to verbalize yet easy to feel and absorb.

For a less jarring introduction to terroir awareness, let us consider the wines of southern France, of the Languedoc, a region of scrub and hills overlooking the Mediterranean. Its sun-burnished slopes swept with patches of wild rosemary, sage, lavender, thyme, tarragon, and wormwood, really do seem able to impart those scents and even flavors to the wines of the interspersed vineyards. In this region as much as any other, one can, while sipping a glass of Fitou or Corbières, easily imagine standing among the stony plots of heather while gazing across a well-tended vineyard to the sparkling Mediterranean beyond.

Not to say that we should smell and taste the local flora in every glass we enjoy, but that a sense of the time and place of any specific wine gives a fuller, more variegated, more complex and complete "reality" to our pleasure. It may be a sense of minerality, of the slate soils and cool climate of the Mosel, or the aging, the precision and respect for the wines of La Rioja.

Consider a wine's time as it fills your mouth and caresses your soul. All those years ago someone walked those slopes and picked the grapes that produced the wine you drink today ... as you fell in

Riesling vineyards overlooking the Mosel River of Germany

love and pledged troth to your spouse, as your brother was struggling to survive a combat tour in foreign lands, while your first child was readying him- or herself to enter the world. These connections of time and space, good or bad, make a wine more significant by introducing the power of memory to the experience of drinking. We are already wired to incorporate memory and flavor; our retro-nasal cavity, which processes aromas and flavors, feeds directly into that portion of the brain that controls memory and emotion. The two are intimately related. It's why the smell of bread baking reminds you of your grandmother or of the summer you spent overseas living next door to a bakery.

Your South African Shiraz was grown in the shadow of Table Mountain in the year you graduated from college. Think about that. At your last wine tasting, one of your group brought a wine made in the year a man first walked on

The heat wave of 2003 produced heavy, short-lived wines.

the moon (1969), and it was terrible, but if you were alive then you likely recalled where you were and what you were doing. Sometime earlier another aficionado shared a bottle of 1950 Bordeaux, made in the year your father was born, and it was stunning, magnificent. As you swirled it in your mouth, not only did you think of the vineyards and cobbled streets of St. Emilion, but you drifted away in thoughts of your father.

Unless you have traveled extensively through the world's wine regions, you won't have much sense of any particular vineyard or topography. But that's nothing a quick online search can't resolve in minutes. A handful of images and a moment to reflect on what was happening in your life, or in that region or in the world at large, during the year of the vintage you're about to consume cannot fail to enrich the experience.

It's not a matter of being all touchy-feely about the wine you consume. It's simply an oenological exercise, this envisioning of time and terroir, to place the moment in context, to slow the persistent swirl of life, to enjoy a mentally and sensually interactive relationship with what others may think of as merely a beverage. But as you know, how wrong they are.

To the vineyards, to the pickers, to the weather. To the great unending procession of life, to all its marvels and mishaps. And to all the vintages yet to come.

TWENTY-EIGHT

T W E N T Y - E I G H T

THROW A WINE DINNER

F EW EVENTS IN THE WORLD OF ENTERTAINING ARE MORE enjoyable than hosting a wine dinner. Wine is, after all, at its best when imbibed with fellow bacchants. The social aspect of wine is hard to overlook; there is something rather marvelous about opening a good/new/untried/untested bottle and sharing it with friends who are as eager as you to give it a whirl. Watch their eyes sometime as you're about to pour.

Something else to love about a wine dinner is that creating a memorable occasion doesn't require a particular size, theme, food, time of year, type of wine, or whatever. It's irrelevant whether you're an expert or still finding your way around the grapevine. It can be done with two wines or four wines or six or eight or ten wines, whatever suits your taste and your budget. It can be formal, catered, delivered, off the grill, or dished up from the Crock-Pot. Truth be told, it's not even necessary to have a table, as long as people can set a plate and a wine glass down somewhere between sips and bites and oohs and aahs (think tailgating, picnics, or relaxing by the pool).

A wine dinner is the ideal opportunity to test a selection of fermented juice and see how well it goes with your favorite foods. Suppose you're a sucker for a bucket of juicy golden fried chicken but have yet to discover the consummate wine to accompany that lovely deep-fried bird. Here is a chance to try. How about starting with a couple of Chardonnays, perhaps a white Cote du Rhone, a Viura (aka white Rioja) and maybe a Bordeaux-style blend of Sémillon and Sauvignon Blanc from Washington state or central California, or, need it be said, Bordeaux, in your search for the "perfect" (to your palate, at least) food and wine pairing.

Think of the possibilities: grilled skirt steak with a duo of Malbecs vs. a left and a right bank Bordeaux; lamb chops with your choice of Syrahs, a bottle of Ribera del Duero, and a solid, salubrious Cabernet Sauvignon; oven-roasted salmon with an array of Oregon Pinot Noir, Alsatian Pinot Gris, and an Italian Soave or two. But these are quick and easy suggestions, pairings that may or may not please you or your friends, and should be given no particular credence. The synergy of wine to food will change, as well, depending on sauces, rubs, or coatings. The point is to 1.) have fun and be social, and 2.) find the wine that *you* like with the food as *you* prefer it prepared.

I have been told of a marvelous wine dinner thrown by a successful restaurateur that featured, under *cloche*, with all those domed, silver covers dramatically removed at the same instant, beautifully arranged plates of tiny, square fast-food burgers. And to everyone's further delight, the wines poured were pricey, well-known, and hard to find. Contrast that scene with a much less formal evening of talk and laughter built around a choice bottle supplied by each guest to accompany the hostess' famous-among-her-friends home-made pizza. The happy result? Barberas, a Carménère, a Dornfelder, Primitivos, and a Cabernet Franc all vying for attention at that very different but equally memorable get-together.

Should you and your guests be serious drinkers of serious wines, put a smile on everyone's wine-stained lips by supplying a tasting sheet and pen or pencil for each attendee. Remember, tailor the evening to the folks you'll be inviting. A less formal group would be amused, or maybe annoyed, at the expectation of scoring and taking notes, while the geeks would bemoan its absence, so prepare accordingly and you will have a happy group.

Some wine dinners are best attended in shorts and flip-flops, while others require a tux and formal attire. Neither is more or less enjoyable, they are simply variations on a theme.

Whether you have been wondering what foods would go best with wines that you already know and love or what wines would be the ideal match for the foods you frequently enjoy, a wine dinner is the party you're looking to throw. And once you do, you'll be surprised at how easy it is and how delightful the experience.

Braised short ribs, spinach lasagna, New England lobster rolls, tofu burgers, rotisserie chicken, pepperoni pizza, hot dogs, caviar, foie gras, veal Marsala, prime rib or Mama's meatloaf, it makes no difference.

Aglianico, Zweigelt, Pinot Noir, Garnacha, Mourvèdre, Merlot, Chenin, Carménère or Pinot Blanc, Picpoul, Pecorino, Marsanne, Gewürztraminer, Torrontés, Tannat or Verdejo, all can and should be tried and compared.

Just cut loose. Pour the wine, serve the food, pour another wine. And then another. Taste, talk, sip, and savor. You'll be glad you did. Your job as the host or hostess is simply to keep the evening moving. Ask about the wine; ask about the food; ask for your guests' impressions of the pairings that work best and why they think one combination is better than another. Everyone's opinion counts, to them at least, so encourage your companions to share their gustatory musings. You'll have a happy and well-fed crew. So here's to you (thanks for the party) and to all the possible pairings!

TWENTY-NINE

TWENTY-NINE

EXPLORE ROSÉS

THERE'S A TIME (USUALLY THOSE MONTHS OF WARMER weather) and a place (outdoors, indoors, wherever one happens to be) for almost everything, and rosé is no exception. These half-white, half-red wines are exploding in popularity. Something about their crisp, light, flavorful, and visually delightful essence is appealing to more and more wine drinkers. While they come in varying levels of sweetness, it's the dry versions that are attracting most of the new adherents.

For too long these lightweight, refreshing sippers were tucked away under the rug of "serious" Old World wines, known only to the fortunate classes who summered along the Mediterranean, toured the towns and castles of the Loire, or visited pockets of northern Spain or southern Italy. Yet rosés are among the most ancient of all wine styles.

Rosés from here, there, and every region imaginable

It has been known for millennia that allowing crushed grapes, with juice, skins, and pulp, to macerate together either before or during fermentation produces a darker, heartier wine. Because most grape juice is clear or very pale, a wine's color and much of its tannin and flavor components are leached from the skins of the grapes. Some cultures simply preferred the less harsh result of minimal skin contact; in other cases, where longer maceration led to higher temperatures, there was always a danger of "stuck" or incomplete fermentations, hence the winemaker's preference for lighter but fully fermented wines.

Fortunately, it's no longer necessary to spend your holidays in Provence or Navarra to enjoy the subtle beauty of these delicious wines. Rosés are now produced in wine regions around the world via one of three different methods. The first we have discussed: a very short period of maceration, ranging from just a few hours to perhaps a day, before the juice is poured off, separated from the grape skins, and fermented. The second technique is referred to by the French term *saignée*, or "bleeding off," a portion of the juice being removed, thereby producing a more intense red wine as the primary product, aiding winemakers who wish to create a wine that is darker and richer than the vintage and the grapes themselves would allow. The excess juice, i.e., that removed from the must, is then fermented without further maceration to create a rosé.

And the simplest, and least regarded method, is to blend red and white wine together, which, some argue, gives the best neither of the red nor of the white wine involved.

Thanks to this greater dispersion of production along with a robust import market, a well-made rosé is seldom far away. It is always a pleasure to enter a well-run wine shop in the spring of the year and see cases and cases of pink-hued rosés from every corner of the globe.

Though many wine lovers consider rosé to be the ideal wine for picnics, summer outings, and warm-weather fare, it is actually a perfect choice whenever one is looking for a lighter, tasty wine with just enough fruit, structure, and personality to go with a wide selection of foods. And speaking of pink-hued ...

Few wines are collectively such a delight for the eyes. Colors, depending on grape variety and length of maceration, run from the palest, luminous onion skin to barely-there salmon to lightly-bruised peach to midwinter-sunset pink to cotton candy to lipstick shades of hot pink and candy-apple red. These are wines that deserve a midday tasting, perhaps an early weekend afternoon, lined up side by side for the sheer joy of seeing them together.

Invite your friends. Tell them all to bring a bottle. So many rosés are on the shelves that it's almost impossible that any two people will bring the same wine. And forget the "real men don't drink pink" baloney. Try using that line around the fishermen of Provence, the bull runners of Pamplona, the dockworkers of southern Italy and see where it gets you. Rosé makes everybody happy!

A sure sign of springtime

You'll find rosés of Grenache, Syrah, Cinsault, Carignan, Mourvèdre, Cabernet Franc, Cabernet Sauvignon, Pinot Noir, Tempranillo, Sangiovese, Barbera, and on and on. They're called *rosados* in Spain and *rosatos* in Italy, and they are made in France, Italy, Spain, the United States, Austria, Australia, Germany, South Africa, Portugal, Argentina, Chile, and Uruguay. And elsewhere. Most are marvelous; a very few are sticky yucky and mass-produced.

Try them alone, or with anything. Don't confuse depth of color with richness of flavor. The palest may be the most intriguing; it simply depends on the specific wines that comprise the lineup. And whether you're a longtime rosé drinker or a newbie to the world of pink wines, chances are good that you're gonna love 'em.

THIRTY
THIRTY

REVIEW SOME ANCIENT HISTORY

A TALL ORDER, TO BE SURE. WITH A HISTORY OF TEN THOUSAND years or more, it's not likely that any of us will, or can, absorb more than a fraction of wine's history and its role in human society and evolution. But we can share the wonder of it, the connection, and the amazement at wine's ancient interaction with the human psyche and state of being.

It's hard to know what happened "prehistory," because, by definition, there are no records to guide us. But we do know that wine was being produced, distributed, valued, and enjoyed for thousands of years, even *before* the invention of writing.

The creation of wine was a simple circumstance. Yet those first few accidental occasions wherein the ambient yeast did their "in with the sugar, out with the wine" routine must have seemed like magic or the workings, the gift, of the gods. From nowhere came this wonderful, powerful, perception-altering beverage. To give warmth where there had been none and to create happiness in place of hardship were its early gifts.

Wine, as anyone who has witnessed the glint of light on a glass of red or has spilled a container of the same can easily understand, soon came to represent blood and, by extension, life and death itself. This, combined with its own mystical origin and the grapes' annual cycle of ripening and renewal, moved it quickly to the center of religious ceremony, from whence it has never strayed.

Untold generations have sipped and smiled and felt the inner glow of wine suffusing their physical and mental selves. When we drink wine, we continue a custom that may date from the Upper Paleolithic. And those pricey stems in which we serve our wine are merely the latest in a long line of vessels used to accommodate our thirst. Our ancestors slurped the gifted juice from their hands, from depressions in rock, from hammered stone bowls, from bags made of animal skins, from watertight bowls woven of reeds and grasses, from hollowed wooden cups, from sunbaked clay, from kiln-fired pottery, from goblets of alabaster and marble, from carefully wrought containers of bronze, silver, and gold, from ivory jars and terra-cotta pots, from finely painted *kylix* and *kraters*, from horn-like *rhytons* as well as from horns themselves, from chalices studded with precious stones, from crude leather tankards, and from untold styles of glassware.

So you, we, are the latest in a continuum of wine drinkers whose number extends back to our Stone Age ancestors, a people amazed and thankful that once again, as in seasons past, their harvest of wild grapes has stewed and bubbled and transformed itself into such a magical, unthinkably marvelous gift.

We've heard, those of us interested in such things, that it was the Phoenicians who traversed the ancient world, spreading both wine culture and grape cuttings. To Greece and Rome. To Spain and France, Sardinia and Sicily, to the northern coast of Africa. And indeed it was, though all this took place millennia after wine's birth and absorption into the very earliest cultures of the Near East. Long after humankind had learned to plant and care for vineyards, to trellis the grapes for easy access at harvest, to crush the newly picked fruit quickly, and to seal the finished drink to protect it from the slow degradation of air.

Put otherwise, it was long after the advent of viticulture and viniculture in the Fertile Crescent that wine reached the Phoenicians. The story of wine was already wrinkled with age by the time the scribes of Sumeria conceived of cuneiform. Priests of the long-lost deities Enki and Marduk, of El, Baal, and Ishtar had for centuries offered wine as a sacrament to their gods; empires had come and gone; and ancient trade routes routinely carried the precious beverage through Armenia, Anatolia, Uruk, and Babylon before wine flowed, finally, into the hands of the Phoenicians on the eastern shores of the Mediterranean.

From there, the Phoenicians dominated the wine trade with Egypt (itself a hotbed of both reds and whites from as early as 3100 BC) and introduced it into Crete (from whence it traveled to mainland Greece) and throughout the Mediterranean. The Greeks in turn carried their vines to the slopes of southern Italy (think of the "modern" varieties Greco di Tufo, Grechetto, and Aglianico, all referring to their origins in the Hellenic lands of Greece), a region so covered in vines as to be known in ancient times as Oenotria, the land of vines.

Just north, in what we now call Tuscany, the Etruscans were renowned for the quality of their wine, until conquered by the Romans and absorbed into that "newer" civilization. To the Romans, wine was a necessity, an essential part of daily life that should be denied no one, not even their slaves. Troops of the empire spread the culture of wine wherever they went, for how could good Romans properly exist in foreign lands without wine to comfort and sustain them?

France, Germany, Austria, Spain—or perhaps more accurately, Gallia, Germania, Noricum, and Hispania—all saw major plantings of vines to satisfy Roman appetites. Where the Phoenicians had focused on coastal areas, the conquering legions carried wines and

vines inland to the mountains and rivers and interiors of these sub-jugated lands. In time, many of the soldiers stayed, took wives from the local populace, and built their lives in these "new" territories. Yet, whether in Rome or the north of Gallia, wine was a commodity of great value on many levels.

There is much to know and much to amaze. If we consider that writing was invented in Mesopotamia about 3200 BC, a bit more than five thousand years ago, it's almost incomprehensible that wine's true "history" extends into the past at least that long *before* writing existed. Maybe longer. Maybe somewhat less.

Ashurbanipal, Assyrian king and conqueror of Babylon, with his queen,
enjoying wine beneath the grapes of the palace garden

An earthen jar containing wine residue and dating to 5400 BC
was unearthed at Hajji Firuz Tepe, a Neolithic village in northern
Iran. It seems that every few years a new discovery pushes the dates
of early wine back further and further.

Of course, it's difficult to learn as much as one might like
about those ancient times and wines. Yet the exploration is rich with
drama, with the commonality of wine lovers from the earliest days.

Ancient records abound with daily wine rations allotted to servants and workers and members of various courts and households.

The builders of the pyramids received both wine and beer as part of their wages; Homer praised the wines of the ancient Minoans; vineyards were planted from Babylon to Nineveh to Jericho and throughout the delta of northern Egypt. Isaiah and Abraham and Pharaoh and King Solomon and even the Queen of Sheba all brought the wine cup to their lips and experienced the same sensation that a swallow of wine excites in us to this day.

There are few easily available sources of such information, but highly recommended are the works of Professor Patrick McGovern of the University of Pennsylvania: *Ancient Wine: The Search for the Origins of Viniculture* and *Uncorking the Past: The Quest for Wine, Beer, and Other Alcoholic Beverages*. The first bit of Hugh Johnson's *The Story of Wine* is also worth the read, as is *Wine: The 8,000 Year–Old Story of the Wine Trade,* by Thomas Pellechia. Other books on the history of agriculture or wine or early civilizations will give you bits and pieces, though once your timeline advances to the cultures of Greece and Rome there is no shortage of records or references or materials to illuminate the place of wine in these "newer" ancient societies and to continue the very long lineage of those who love wine—as a sacrament, as a beverage, as a welcome reward. *Şerefe!*

THIRTY-ONE

THIRTY-ONE

DRINK THE WINES OF YOUR OWN STATE OR REGION—OR DON'T

THIS CHAPTER ISN'T MEANT TO BE CONTRADICTORY. IT IS, in fact, a call to exploration. Too many wine drinkers in the United States who routinely enjoy the juice of Europe, Australia, or South America have seldom, or never, tried the wines of their own states. Of course, most residents of California, Washington, Oregon, and possibly New York can be excluded from this larger group and will fall under the "or Don't" portion of the above title.

But what of the wine lovers in Cincinnati who have never picnicked by the banks of the Ohio sipping a dry Traminette; the denizens of D.C. who wouldn't know a Norton if they fell into a barrel of it? Newport swells unfamiliar with the local Vidal Blanc; grape nuts of St. Louis who've never tasted Chardonel; North Carolinians with no idea of the lovely Chambourcin being turned out just down the road?

This shouldn't be taken as an unqualified endorsement of the hybrids and non-vinifera grape varieties found throughout much of the central and eastern United States (though the general improvements in winemaking science and equipment have affected these grapes as much as any other) but as a call to familiarize wine drinkers with their local product. Some of which is remarkably good.

Not every winery outside the major production areas has a need for clones or hybrids or native varieties that can withstand extreme cold or fend off regional fungal or insect invasions. *Vitis vinifera* is alive and well from sea to shining sea. How many Bostonians are aware that excellent Chardonnay is being produced within fifty miles of their historic city? And how many Texans realize how easy it's become to lay hands on a terrific Lone Star-made Viognier or Cabernet Sauvignon? Who knew that a family from Champagne would set up shop in New Mexico and start producing high-quality sparkling wines, that Colorado is home to a legion of kick-ass Syrahs, or that Michigan can boast more than one quite nicely done Pinot Grigio?

But maybe you *are* from California or New York; maybe you drink your state's grape juice, be it Merlot, Zinfandel, Cabernet Sauvignon, Cab Franc, or Riesling, on a regular basis (as well you should). However, what do you know about Walla Walla or Loudon County? How much Barolo or Sagrantino crosses your lips? Is Sicily in your sights, or in your cellar? Do you sample Viuras, Txakolis, or Roditis occasionally?

We all get into rhythms and routines. When we live in a region famous for producing outstanding wine, it's easy to forget there are other sources of equally superb juice—that's different, compelling, and delicious—beyond the borders of the surrounding restaurants and wine shops. And when that's the case, it benefits your palate, your knowledge, and your experience of wine to *not* always drink the local wine but instead to explore the wines of other locales, the everyday selections of wine lovers who live in some other place. This is where the "or Don't" comes into play.

If home is San Francisco, why not forgo the usual Merlot, Cabernet, or Petite Sirah and try what the average family in Naples or Vienna or Zagreb might drink? Portland is awash in (world-class) Pinot Noir, but if you drink what's *not* local, you might enjoy a wine that Greeks or Spaniards or Argentineans imbibe on a regular basis, a wine you may not be familiar with, an excellent well-made wine, a wine with a different taste profile, and perhaps a new variety to bolster your oenological database.

It's the tasting and the trying, the enjoyment and assessment of wines from around the world that broadens our palates, that provides a more engaged sense of wine as a shared human experience. A Xinomavro with roast leg of lamb recalls a family meal in northern Greece. Fried or grilled branzino with a chilled Verdicchio connects you to food- and wine-loving Italians living along the Adriatic coast.

Just as it behooves Americans to experience that which they usually overlook, so does it serve the wine experience of citizens of other lands to shake off the dust of the familiar and reach out into the world of wines unknown. What a prize Rioja holds in store for the Milanese, or Negroamaro for a resident of Burgundy.

It's true that in many countries the availability of "foreign" wines is greatly limited. While Chileans would be forced to search hither and yon to locate a Pinot Noir from Central Otago and Athenians would have no easy task comparing an Albariño with an Assyrtiko, even the Bordelais have limited access to wines of the Rhone, and Cabernet Sauvignons from Western Australia are not so common in the Cab-centric region of Coonawarra in South Australia.

All one can do, then, is ask local merchants to stock more of those "outside wines," to give customers access to the best of the best, regardless of their origin—and then to support them when they do. The world of wine is large and multifaceted. It makes sense that restaurants and wine shops in established regions feature their local wines above those they have to import or pay extra duties and transportations costs to obtain. Yet it's through the very diversity of the wine experience, trying options from here, there, and somewhere else that drinkers become fans, and fans in turn become aficionados. And really now, isn't *aficionado* just another word for *lover*? *Gān Bēi!*

THIRTY-TWO
THIRTY-TWO

DO A TASTING OF SWEET NON-DESSERT WINES

S WEET WINES HAVE BEEN AROUND FOR AS LONG AS WINE itself; in fact, one could make the case that the first wines were probably sweet, or at least sweeter than most of us are used to drinking. Though the current style of wines, excepting intentionally sweet dessert wines, leans heavily to dry, fully fermented versions, this has not always been the case.

As recently as the 1950s, 70% of California's wine production was sweet. South Africa has a long history of sweet non-dessert winemaking; sweet Vouvray is one of the Loire Valley's best-known wines; Germany's top-tier Rieslings were and are known for their sweetness; Champagne was historically sweet, and a portion of it remains so; Italians are fond of their Moscato d'Asti, Lambrusco, and off-dry Prosecco; and Australia generates a bevy of sweet Shiraz.

That sweetness comes from the residual sugar remaining after fermentation, though alcohol itself has a sweet taste as well. Hence, wines with higher alcohol often seem a bit sweeter than others—a situation that may be intended or accidental. While the nature of yeast is to consume and convert all the sugar in their environment into CO_2 and alcohol, the process can be halted at any point by heating, cooling, or adding spirits to the fermenting must. Thus the winemaker has a great ability to control the sweetness level of her product.

When temperatures are too cool, say in the low 50's F (a cool autumn day in the foothills of the Caucasus Mountains), yeast become sluggish and cease doing their job. When temperatures climb into the 90's F, yeast are damaged and simply cannot consume. And when late-harvest grapes with excess sugar content push alcohol levels above 14% or 15% the yeast are killed off and don't work at all. For these and other reasons, many ancient wines were never fully fermented and were instead prized for their sweetness.

But history and fermentation aside, there are two good reasons to conduct a tasting of sweet (non-dessert) wines. First, there are more sweet wines around than most folks realize, and ignoring them means missing a significant category of wine that is drunk and enjoyed worldwide. No matter how dry most current wines are, a not insignificant percentage of sippers are happy to at least try the sweeter stuff.

And second, more people than might be imagined—not all people but a lot of people—love them! That probably includes people in your own circle of friends and fellow drinkers. It has been estimated that as much as 20% of the population prefers their wines sweet, but who's to know whether you or your compatriots are among that percentage if you never give the wines a try?

The wine world's current focus on dry fermentations, coupled with an unfortunate look-down-the-nose attitude of many wine geeks and so-called professionals toward sweet wine in general, has scared many would-be wine drinkers into the periphery. Instead of voicing their preference for the sweet stuff, many have opted for cocktails and mixed drinks in place of wine, or they hide a bottle of Moscato in the reefer to be pulled out when no one "in the know" happens to be visiting.

Think about that as you start putting together your guest list for the big tasting. At the same time, don't be surprised when a friend who has been into wine for years confesses that he or she has always loved sweet wine but thought it inappropriate to pull out a bottle of the stuff in "sophisticated" wine company.

Should you want snacks, or something more substantial to pair with your selection of sweet stuff, there is no shortage of foods that go well with a little sugar in the accompanying beverage. Start your tasting with Champagne (always an excellent approach to launching a wine event) labeled demi-sec, sec, or extra sec and, perhaps to nibble, something crunchy with a sprinkling of salt. Both the sweetness and the bubbles will come to life when paired with texture and a bit of saltiness.

Just to provide some context, sweetness (i.e., residual sugar) in wine is usually expressed either in grams per liter (g/l) or as a percentage. Accordingly, the standards for wine are as follows:

Table Wine	
bone-dry	1 g/l <
dry	1-10 g/l
off-dry	10-35 g/l
sweet	35-120 g/l
very sweet (dessert)	> 120 g/l

Champagne & Sparkling	
brut	0-12 g/l
extra sec	12-17 g/l
sec (dry)	17-32 g/l
demi-sec	32-50 g/l
doux (rare)	> 50 g/l

These are not legal standards, nor do they often appear on wine labels, but they will give you a sense of how much sugar may or may not be in that bottle you're about to open.

The first level, that of bone-dry, is seldom achieved, as there remain small amounts of unfermentable sugars in all wines. In fact, most dry wine contains up to 4 g/l, a level the average taster can barely discern. Winemakers often choose to leave this minimal amount in their wine, as it gives weight and a fuller mouthfeel to the wine. Generally speaking, New and Old World philosophies differ on this approach, as can be evidenced by tasting a number of dry, everyday cuvées from France, Italy, or Spain and then switching to a lineup of dry American or other New World wines. The difference will be startling. Neither is better or worse; they simply illustrate cultural variance.

Before returning to the wines for a sweet (non-dessert) tasting, one further point is useful as far as fully understanding the topic at hand. The *perception* of sweetness is greatly affected by the level of acid in a wine, and vice versa. A glass of water with five or six spoonsful of sugar in it would seem markedly sweet, but stir the same amount of sugar into a mix of lemon juice and water and behold—a lovely glass of lemonade!

Wines like Champagne and Riesling are noted for high acidity, and so their sweetness, while noticeable, isn't likely to be overwhelming. As a result, these wines may have broader appeal than some others that might be included in your tasting.

You may, in addition to a sec or demi-sec Champagne, wish to add a Moscato d'Asti, Asti Spumante, Lambrusco, or sparkling Shiraz, all sweet or slightly sweet sparklers that should be fairly easy to obtain. Brachetto and Prosecco, two other Italian *frizzantes*, one red and one white, made in both sweet and dry versions, are also worth considering. These lightly sweet options go beautifully with fruit. Something with pears or possibly a wheel of baked brie with a fruit topping would be delicious.

Once past the bubblies and into the whites, still Moscato may be all the rage, but for a more complex experience don't leave out the Riesling, Gewürztraminer, or Chenin Blanc. All three are produced in Old and New World locales, so the options are many. Off-dry (code for sorta sweet) Riesling is well-made and well-known in the Pacific Northwest, some of the best coming from Washington state. The standard for sweet Old World Riesling hail from Germany; look in particular for bottles labeled *Spätlese* or *Auslese* for a definite but manageable dose of sugar. These are beautiful wines with tons of personality and lots of acid, loved by even the most aren't-we-cool-just-ask-us fanciers of the grape.

Gewürztraminer, a floral, lychee, spicy glass of wonderful, is less informative in its labeling. It might be wise to enlist the aid of your local wine merchant to separate the off-dry from the dry. Never a big seller, though why not is hard to say, Gewürz is vinified in Alsace, Italy, and Austria, and in smaller amounts in Spain, Hungary, Canada, Chile, Argentina, Australia, and the United States, to name but a few. It's a big wine, deeper in color and higher in alcohol than Riesling. A good bottle is an experience not to be missed.

Another long-loved sweet wine claims the Loire Valley of France as its home, though South Africa has likewise turned out both sweet and dry versions of Chenin Blanc for many years. The best of the French versions are labeled Vouvray, while their African cousins go simply by Chenin Blanc (or Steen if you prefer the now-mostly-out-of-favor name that may or may not incur the wrath of the Cape Winelands' exceptionally skilled winemakers) and in both instances the assistance of your wine seller will help separate the sweet from the dry. All three, Riesling, Chenin, and Gewürztraminer, use their touch of sweetness to good effect in pairing with complex, hot and spicy Thai, Indian, or Cajun foods, in particular.

And let us not overlook the big red brethren. While it is unfortunately true that most in the United States commandery of wine correctness yet maintain their prejudice against sweet reds, there is, as they say, more than one way to skin a grape. One approach is simply to go elsewhere, Australia being a good place to begin. Shiraz is often made in a big, blowsy, very ripe style that retains a healthy dose of residual sugar. Beyond that is the intentionally sweet style of Shiraz, with an even higher percentage of sugar. And, of course, the aforementioned Lambrusco and Brachetto of Italy are both red and sweet as well. Again, ask your wine merchant which are most likely to fill your needs.

While we're in overseas mode, exploring the secret corners of former Soviet wine culture (where sweet reds have long been well-regarded) may yield even more results. Hungary, in particular, is proud of its semi-sweet Blaufränkisch, a variety otherwise known as one of Austria's premium dry wines. And from what may be the original home of winemaking, it's becoming ever easier to find Georgian wines on U.S. shelves, specifically Kindzmarauli, a product of the Saperavi grape, and the historic blend called Khvanchkara, made of two semi-sweet reds with ancient lineage.

A second approach to skirting anti-sweet-red sentiment is going through the back door, i.e. laying mitts on some full-blown high-alcohol Zinfandels from California. These often have noticeable levels of sugar, their sweetness accentuated by high levels of alcohol. But not only can "respectable" wines be stuffed with candy, anyone willing to cross the vinous tracks to the wrong side of wine town can now find generic "sweet reds" from a number of the large wine companies. These are hardly award winners, but their presence does indicate a growing demand for a little sugar among a certain segment of wine drinkers.

Whether served with barbecued ribs, hot wings, or spicy nachos, all these reds are worth a sip and a swallow. Get the group together and have fun, nothing serious, just a plain old good time. You might be surprised at which of your friends are the really sweet ones!

THIRTY-THREE
THIRTY-THREE

VOLUNTEER TO WORK CRUSH

THE INSIDE TRACK IS ALWAYS THE PLACE TO BE. WHETHER it's riding with the band on the tour bus, sharing the team bench on the sidelines of the championship game, or dining at the chef's table in the season's hottest restaurant, the fun factor is exponentially amped up when you're part of the action and not just another observer.

Think about it: from the inside you get a feel for how the show really works, for the jobs and responsibilities that count, that make everything happen. The inside track comes with access to insights and information not available to most, the opportunity to interact with the principals, to see it all—the big picture *and* the details from their perspective, to have your questions answered and probably to walk away from the experience with something extra, something a visit by itself would never provide.

It's been said that to profit from a relationship, determine first how to help someone else get what he or she needs or desires. Only then should one hope for anything in return. For the farmer, aka the vigneron, who is perpetually understaffed at harvest time, help is often hard to come by. In any seasonal endeavor, securing adequate labor when it's needed can be a challenging proposition. For a vineyard where the grapes are handpicked—still the majority, though labor costs and shortages are forcing more and more wineries to consider mechanical harvesting—having enough bodies in the vineyards and on the crush pad when the grapes *must* be brought in is critical to the success of the vintage. Remember, this is fruit; when it's ripe it's ripe. Any delay in picking, even a day or two, can push Brix levels too high and drop acid levels too low.

The solution? Short-term harvest help, long a staple in wineries worldwide. In many regions, wineries depend on local and not so local volunteers to supply the extra hands needed to pick and sort and do many of the other tasks required to get the grapes in and the fermentation started and keep the place clean. More than a few wine fans look back on their season(s) picking or sorting grapes in France or Spain or the rolling hills of Oregon with great affection. Of such experiences are lifelong memories made.

In the most casual of situations, any help at all is welcome. Some volunteers may work only for a weekend or a handful of days. At the other end of the red, white, and sparkly spectrum is ten or twelve weeks of long days, sore backs, and tired fingers. If this sounds like your kind of adventure, by all means pursue it. Seeing the winery operation from the inside, being part of it, is to immerse yourself in a long history of human undertaking, in the camaraderie of shared effort and learning.

You might stand at the sorting table with the son or daughter of a famous winemaker from Australia, hose down the winery floor with a college professor on sabbatical, swap stories with an attorney from your hometown, or meet a wine lover like yourself visiting from a small town on the outskirts of Vienna. You will definitely become

Napa Valley, volunteers at the sorting table

reacquainted with the restorative pleasure of a long hot bath at the end of the day—if you can stay awake that long.

As all this work requires fuel, most wineries feed their crews very well, usually with a liberal contribution of the winery's own product. For those who enjoy it, "working crush" is an eagerly awaited annual event, something many folks look forward to year after year.

Wineries in the United States generally begin signing up harvest help in January or February, hoping to fill out their rosters by the time their grapes are ripe in late summer. There are web sites and portals that list some of these positions, but it's just as easy to pick up the phone and call or send an e-mail expressing your interest to the winery of your choice. And don't think it's just small or second-tier operations that look for seasonal workers. Every winery needs to get its fruit in, and these positions can be had at wineries from the most famous to the least well known.

You should be aware there are changes afoot in the volunteer community. In certain regulatory-burdened states, labor officials are casting a jaundiced eye on volunteers who choose to donate their time without pay. This means, in turn, that wineries in those regions are now forced to pay wages to their short-term harvest help.

Of course, wineries continue to need the extra hands, backs, and bodies; that hasn't changed, as grapes still need picking and the show must go on—unfortunately at greater expense to the

Harvest crew dinner is a regular event at many wineries.

winery—and most are eager to enlist the services of the smiling faces who might previously have joined them as volunteers. Now, however, those "volunteers" may be forced to accept a paycheck. Could be worse, one imagines.

Whether as volunteer or short-term hire, if the work, friendships, and excitement of being a winery insider appeal to your adventurous nature, this can be a wonderful way to try your hand as a cellar rat and come home with stories and friends and a new respect for the work of making wine that will last a lifetime. Happy trails, and enjoy every minute of it.

THIRTY-FOUR

THIRTY-FOUR

ADD *RETSINA, KVEVRI* TO YOUR VOCABULARY

N OT TO MENTION *TINAJA, PITHOS,* AND *AMPHORA.* WHICH, along with *kvevri,* are ancient terra-cotta fermentation and storage vessels, still used in scattered locales and actually growing in popularity. Having survived the evolutions and revolutions of time, and all the "advances and improvements" in the art and science of winemaking, modern eyes, minds, and palates are re-examining these historic containers and their intriguing impact on the wines made and stored within them.

Baked clay being a porous material, various methods and substances were used to reduce spoilage and evaporation of the wines stored and transported in these "pots," a serious and persistent problem. The most common solution of the ancient world was to coat the inner surfaces, or the stoppers or covers used to seal them, with some variety of resin or pine tar. The resulting resinated wine took on some of the flavor of the applied pine pitch, much as modern wines incorporate flavors derived from the oak barrels in which they are stored. In Greece, this wine came to be known as retsina. While its taste is definitely an acquired one, retsina is still quite popular— an easily obtainable link to wine as may have been sipped by Plato while hard at work on revisions to the *Republic*, or a youthful Alexander the Great plotting his conquest of the Persian Empire.

Clearly, not all the wines of yore would be as pleasing to contemporary tasters. There is little question that much of what passed as wine in millennia gone by was downright nasty. Dreck, at best. One can imagine that much of it would have been cloudy, oxidized, and oddly flavored with additives like sea water, lead, pepper, and thyme, used in large part to offset the aroma and taste of wine going bad.

And yet the ancients spoke of particular wines with near reverence. It was said that more than one Middle Eastern potentate cellared remarkable vintages, best enjoyed after many years of aging. Homer extolled the wines of the Aegean islands of Chios, Limnos, and Lesbos. Pliny the Elder praised the Pompeiana wines of Campania, describing them as "full-bodied and robust," improving with age and best around ten years old. The 121 BC vintage of Falernian, regarded as one of the greatest of all time (sound familiar?), was served to Caesar with much applause sixty-one years later to celebrate his conquest of Iberia—and was said to still be drinkable, though clearly past its prime, into its second century. The Egyptian writer Athenaeus waxed poetic about Mareotis, about its "excellent quality and sweet and fragrant bouquet," declaring it superior to all other wines of the combined kingdoms. And on and on, from Mesopotamia to the peak of the Roman Empire.

So while some wines, maybe most, were of dubious quality, many, it seems, were quite pleasing to the palates of their day. And while technology advanced and barrels and wine presses, and then chemicals and mechanization, invaded the world of oenology, there remained pockets of traditional techniques and processes that stuck to the way things had always been done.

Folks in the Caucasus Mountains and on the plains of Spain, for instance, make wine much as their ancestors have for a very long time; in the case of those winemakers located between the Caspian and Black Seas, as long as eight thousand years. Hard to conceive of, perhaps, but this region that now consists of the Republics of Georgia and Armenia, northwestern Iran, and eastern Turkey is generally acknowledged to be the birthplace of wine and winemaking—start date unknown but ten thousand-plus years is not unlikely.

Here the vessel of choice is the *kvevri* (alternate spelling: *qvevri*), best-described as the Sumo wrestler of clay amphorae. These monster jars, their inner surfaces often coated with beeswax to prevent oxidation, hold from one hundred to five hundred gallons or more, and are buried neck-deep in the ground. Crushed grapes: skins, stems, seeds and all are thrown in and left to ferment without additions or assistance.

Georgia on my mind

Red wines may be racked off into smaller *kvevri* after fermentation, but then both reds and whites are sealed in their terra-cotta sleeping chambers for six-plus months of undisturbed aging. The result is a beautiful, complex star-bright liquid that has matured with minimal intervention. Thanks to its shape, the *kvevri* allows all the attributes of extended lees contact without reductive or sulfurous notes tainting the wine; solid matter settles into the small conical bottom so as to have little direct contact with the wine itself. The earth provides just the right temperature for both fermentations and storage. The reds are rich and robust; the whites are powerful, orange-hued, with noticeable tannins. These are, in every sense, natural wines.

On the dry, scorched plains of La Mancha, an almost identical Spanish version of *kvevri*, there known as *tinajas*, have been used, if not for millennia certainly for centuries. Sometimes fully buried as are *kvevri*, sometimes partially or not at all, they were, until recently, regarded as mere throwbacks to less modern times. Only now are those on the leading edge of Spanish oenology appreciating *tinajas'* great value, especially in maintaining constant temperatures in an area prone to extreme heat in summer and bone-chilling cold in winter.

One group, the vignerons of Montilla-Moriles in Jerez, have long appreciated the uniqueness and positive impact of *tinajas* on their range of wines, from dry-as-can-be Finos to the unctuous, profoundly sweet Pedro Ximénez.

Ancient-styled, low-intervention wines have a growing audience and an ever-increasing coterie of adherents. Consider a dirt vessel (terra-cotta being a product of clay) sunk into the earth and encased by the existing terrain of soil and rocks and whatever organic matter is to be found, with naught but grapes and grape stems within, allowed to ferment as naturally as possible and to produce wine in its purest, most elemental form.

The return to this philosophy includes winemakers' utilizing amphorae, *pithos* (an ancient style of Greek wine jar) and other natural vessels with grapes macerating on their own skins and seeds

Terra-cotta, Spanish-style

for extended periods of time within the embrace of Mother Earth, yielding complex, tannic, balanced wines of amazing personality and interest. No small feat, this. And all without inoculations, additions, tweaking, or treatments by the winemakers involved.

These ancient methods until recently teetered on the brink of extinction but now are thankfully being "rediscovered" by adventurous winemakers around the world as the overall move away from artificial and interventionist winemaking continues to build momentum. Spain had seen fewer and fewer *tinajas*; *pithos* and amphorae were little more than museum pieces; retsina had become a cheap curiosity, bad wine made with second-rate fruit. And no one even knew, or much less cared about, what was going on in Georgia under control of the former Soviet Union.

But the Greeks always had a taste for retsina, part of their heritage for at least two or three thousand years. As they returned to the world wine stage, a forward-looking generation of winemakers upped the ante and began using good-quality fruit and dialing back on the amount, and intensity, of pine resin.

And the Spanish realized that while modern stainless steel tanks and fermenters with automatic cooling jackets do the job, their respect for tradition inspired a serious look back and a renewed appreciation for the natural low-cost temperature control of their *tinajas*.

Kvevri winemaking is not simply a tradition still in favor among a certain cadre of Georgians. It is ingrained in the culture, widespread in towns and villages across the country. In citing this ancient technique (inscribed on the United Nations' List of the Intangible Cultural Heritage of Humanity), UNESCO had this to say:

> *Most farmers and city dwellers use this method of making wine. Wine plays a vital role in everyday life and in the celebration of secular and religious events and rituals. Wine cellars are still considered the holiest place in the family. The tradition of Qvevri winemaking defines the lifestyle of local*

communities and forms an inseparable part of their cultural identity and inheritance, with wine and vines frequently evoked in Georgian oral traditions and songs.

All around the world, in corners of Italy, Austria, Germany, France, Chile, Australia and even the United States, clay is back. Whether called *kvevri, tinajas, amphorae, dolia,* or some other term from antiquity, whether buried up to their necks, only halfway, or maintained entirely aboveground, they seem, when utilized properly, to result in wines with clean, appealing, and unique aromas, remarkable complexity, and a surfeit of personality.

Azienda Agricola Elisabetta Foradori

The only thing left to do is try them. And while indulging, to be mindful that *kvevri* date back six or eight thousand years to the region that once produced the bulk of prehistoric wine, wine that traversed ancient trade routes to the kings and priests of Babylon and Mesopotamia and the wealthy and influential of Canaan and Byblos. And always, spoilage or oxygenation was a problem. Jars and bags, and eventually amphorae, were stoppered with reeds and twigs and plugs of wood wrapped in clay. At some point, resin began to be used, both to coat the insides of the vessels and to seal their closures. Over time, certain cultures, as mentioned, became acclimated to the flavor, just as contemporary drinkers appreciate the organoleptic influence of oak on much of the wine we drink today.

And now, thousands of years later, we have the opportunity to enjoy styles and cuvées that even the ancients would (might?) recognize. Starting with the piney, floral, lemony retsina that matches so well with strong-tasting foods like garlic and feta, look for the best of the new wave, the resinated wines of Gaia or Papagiannakos, Domaine Vassiliou or Ino. You may have to search—ask your retailer, use the Internet, or look for the Greek grocery nearest you.

Wineries and winemakers experimenting with terra-cotta include Josko Gravner and Paolo Vodopivec of Friuli-Venezia Giulia, in northeast Italy; Elisabetta Foradori from nearby Trentino; and Azienda Agricola COS and Frank Cornelissen of Sicily. From Spain come the untamed offerings of Bodegas Bernabé, from Germany those of Weingut Peter Jakob Kühn. Austria contributes Weingut Bernhard Ott, New Zealand is home to Pyramid Valley and in the United States A.D. Beckham, a ceramicist and winemaker, makes his own terra-cotta fermenters. Though just a sampling, these are among the easiest of this new old wave of wines to find.

These are wines of character and complexity. White or red, they benefit from decanting. Think power, and flavors not in line with those you are used to. Many of these winemakers employ radically noninterventionist techniques in addition to the use of clay vessels; they may eschew the use of fertilizers, pesticides, sulfur. Imagine wine when the

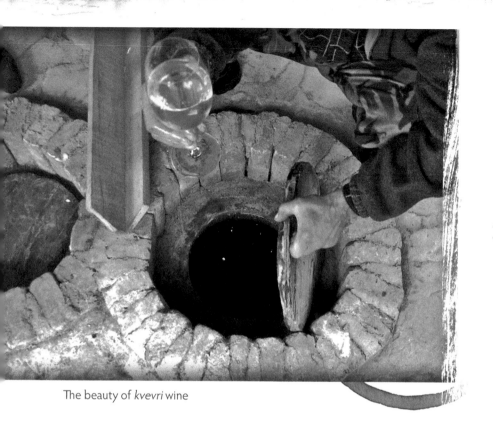

The beauty of *kvevri* wine

weather and its partner in mischief, Dionysius, controlled the outcome of every vintage. These are wines that push the boundaries.

Of course, that leaves the Georgians, keepers of the flame, the
"mustn't be missed." The *kvevri* wines of Georgia are in short supply in much of the world; their export economy is limited, and most
wine made in the age-old tradition is still the product of families and
smaller wineries. Fortunately, both good and stunning examples of
kvevri wines do, increasingly, make their way to the marketplace.

In searching the retailers and websites that champion these
cuvées, look for Pheasant's Tears, for Shaluri Cellars and Vinoterra,
for Orgo Winery (the project of *kvevri* master Gogi Dikishivili and
his son Temur), Gotsa Family, and always for the wines of Alaverdi
Monastery, spiritual center of the Georgian wine universe. The
varieties you will see most often are the whites Kisi, Mtsvane, and
Rkatsiteli, and the reds Saperavi and Shavkapito.

Drink these as you would contemplate an event of great import. We tend too quickly to toss the factory- or mass-produced fermentations of lovely vineyards down our thirsty throats. Think instead of eons of grateful humans offering thanks for the embrace of the elixir of gods and earth and wind and rain and sunshine upon our faces. *Gaumaržos!*

THIRTY-FIVE
THIRTY-FIVE

LOOK UNDER THE REGIONAL RUGS

ANY DISCUSSION OF PIEMONTE, THE FAMED WINE REGION of northern Italy, touches on Barolo and Barbaresco, pinnacles of the Nebbiolo grape, as well as Barbera and Dolcetto, wonderful reds intended for delicious everyday consumption. White wine lovers have long been enamored of the wines of Gavi (thanks to the grape Cortese) and, more recently, Arneis, while fans of sparkling wines enjoy the sweet low-alcohol Moscato d'Asti.

But how often does the conversation veer to Brachetto or Grignolino, two vibrant, fruity, and refreshing Piemonte reds or, on the white side, Erbaluce, more than worthy of exploration and a place on the summertime wine list?

When speaking of Argentina, especially the Mendoza region, all the talk is of Malbec, a wine assuredly deserving of attention. Dense and complex, with rich blackberry and mulberry flavors and its distinctive undercurrent of minerality, this French transplant has become the big kahuna of the eastern slope of the Andes. Perhaps now and again Cabernet Sauvignon is mentioned, as some classic examples of this variety are produced here as well, but how often is the varietal name Bonarda uttered, though it's the second-most widely planted grape of the region? The best wines of this usually overlooked variety are redolent with smoke and leather, spice and violets, yet we hardly see it, whether on retail store shelves or the wine lists of our favorite restaurants.

Every region has a reputation, some international and others decidedly local, tied to the grapes and wines for which it is best known. In much of the Old World this connection is by decree—appellations are strictly regulated, especially in terms of which grape varieties may or may not be included in a particular wine or even planted within the boundaries of the appellation. The so-called New World, on the other hand, has a welcome dearth of restrictive covenants, either in or outside of legally delineated appellations. In most of these non-Euro wine regions reputations are based on a three-legged stool of quality, popularity, and marketing.

Think Napa Valley and most will think Cabernet Sauvignon and perhaps Chardonnay; think Barossa Valley and thoughts turn automatically to Shiraz. Even in the Old World, Tuscany is synonymous with Sangiovese (whether in the form of Chianti, Brunello di Montalcino or Vino Nobile di Montepulciano); the versatile Loire with Cabernet Franc (be it from Anjou, Bourgueil, Saumur, or Chinon), Chenin Blanc (Savennières, Vouvray and others), Sauvignon Blanc (best-known from the appellations of Pouilly-Fumé and Sancerre), and Melon de Bourgogne (aka Muscadet). In a way, this all makes perfect sense, as it provides a reference point for wine buyers, wine dealers, retailers, tourists, and so on.

But how many wine sippers expect to stumble across Grenache or Tempranillo or even Albariño in California's Cab-and-Chardonnay-dominant Napa Valley? Or uncover a steely Riesling or full-bodied Sémillon in Australia's Barossa Valley; or to find such a thing as Loire Gamay or white Arbois?

Understanding this, it's possible to see how lesser-known appellations, varieties, or even "rogue" wineries or vineyards are often lost to everyday discussion or consideration. Wine lovers interested in something from New Zealand might naturally reach for one of their exuberant Sauvignon Blancs, or a well-done Pinot Noir, or possibly one of many excellent Chardonnays, all of which are fairly easy to locate. But how many wine heads are familiar with the island nation's Syrahs, done in a peppery, cool-climate style reminiscent of the northern Rhone?

Oenophiles with a basic knowledge of Hungarian wine are likely to be fans of Tokaji, one of the world's great dessert wines, with a long history of being drunk by the kings and monarchs, the elites and cognoscenti of European empires, from King Louis XIV of France to Austrian Emperor Franz Joseph to Madame de Pompadour to Queen Victoria to Voltaire and Fredrick the Great and, of course, Ludwig van Beethoven, to name but a few.

And haven't we all heard of Bull's Blood, the lusty red blend that so impressed outside invaders, specifically the forces of Suleiman the Magnificent, driven off in 1552 by Hungarian defenders who, it was rumored, daily drank the blood of bulls mixed with the local red wine to give themselves the strength and determination of those powerful bovines? Well, surely Tokaji and Bull's Blood, both still dominant on today's Hungarian drinks menu, are the wines most associated with this central European nation. But how many drinkers have dug deeper and discovered the glories of dry Furmint, a key variety in Tokaji that is increasingly fermented to a bone-dry, almost Riesling-like intensity? It is a wine growing in popularity, in certain geekish circles, and maybe one that your friends and fellow imbibers are not yet familiar with.

All well and good, you say, but how does one go about unearthing these treasures? Or even discover there are treasures to be unearthed? Stores carry what they will, and exotic, little-known wines aren't usually part of the inventory. And truth be told, wine lists outside major metropolitan areas are too often uninspired composites of California Cabernet, Merlot, and Chardonnay, with a few Bordeaux, Italian, and/or Spanish selections thrown in to clear the distributors' shelves and lend a touch of "worldliness" to the list.

This may be so, but a genuine wine lover is not about to be discouraged by the sad state of everyday wine lists and run-of-the-mill retailers. In fact, the tides of commerce are in your favor as it becomes more and more de rigueur among wine sellers of all sorts to offer the newly discovered, the little-known, the hidden gems or the recently saved from extinction. It has actually become fashionable to offer at least a few esoteric bottles. Prod and question the people who normally sell the wines that you buy. You will probably realize, once again, that many wine merchants and beverage directors are as interested and excited about these "fringe" wines as you are. And with a little effort, you can supply them with the specifics of what you would like to try.

Simply research "the wines of ... " or "the grapes of ... " just about any wine region, anywhere, and you'll uncover some real surprises. Whether in print or online, most of the information you seek is easily available. Should you live in an area with few good wine shops to be found, there's an abundance of excellent retailers on the Internet who will gladly ship orders of only a bottle or two to most parts of the world.

How else to discover the Grechetto of Umbria, the Pinot Noir of Casablanca Valley, the Mandilaria of Rhodes, the Aligoté of Burgundy, the Tinta Barroca of Stellenbosch, the Alicante Bouschet of Alentejo, or the Petit Verdot of Napa Valley? So many at-least-interesting, at-most-stunning wines are routinely overlooked by the average wine lover. Pedro Ximénez from the Elqui Valley? (Not to be confused with Pedro Jimenez, also grown in Chile and used primarily in the production of pisco. Okay, okay. It's confusing.) Merlot from Tuscany? Grenache Blanc from Lodi? Yes, yes, and yes. To begin with. And in fact, it's always rather exciting to be confronted with a grape varietal or wine style you never knew existed.

Oh, put on your explorers' hats, my friends. Poke and pry and lift the regional rugs to see what lies beneath. Don't let custom or habit or the marketing folks determine what you will and won't. This is wine, after all, and gifted winemakers encircle the globe. Find something new, different, delicious, and fun. And unexpected! Raise high your vinous sabers and proclaim victory over the commonplace. The world of wine awaits your arrival. Dispatch, if you will, the same old same-old.

THIRTY-SIX

THIRTY-SIX

THROW A BLENDING PARTY

T HERE AREN'T MANY THINGS MORE FUN, CHALLENGING, OR instructive in the world of wine appreciation than having a go at blending. The combining of one wine with another to create a whole that exceeds the sum of its parts is a gift, a gauntlet thrown, and a great way to spend an evening with wine-loving friends of the proactive variety.

At its simplest, for example, blending three or four percent Viognier (a white) into Syrah (a red—very unusual to blend red and white) to lift the wine's aromatics and make it more approachable, as has been done in the premier northern Rhone appellation of Côte-Rôtie for many years, is rather straightforward (though, in fact, the blending is usually of the grapes before fermentation). A touch of this into a lot of that can make the final product "better" than had it been left alone.

A surprising amount of the wine we drink is a blend of various grapes and sometimes even vintages. Bordeaux, Rioja, Chianti, Châteauneuf-du-Pape, Valpolicella, and others are all comprised of two, three or four, or as many as thirteen allowable varieties (in the case of Châteauneuf-du-Pape). In Champagne, the art of blending reaches its zenith with an average bottling assembled from perhaps thirty, fifty, or more different wines. The masters behind this handiwork not only taste the individual wines as they are at the moment but, more important, project how they will taste, as a blend, after a second fermentation *and* three or four years of aging on their lees. Clearly, it takes years of experience and a highly trained palate to achieve this level of vinous virtuosity.

Snazzy glassware

Fortunately, no such prerequisites are required for an afternoon or evening with a group of friends blending your own good, bad, or marvelous cuvées. You will, however, need a few supplies: a graduated cylinder, a beaker or conical flask, and a pipette for each blender. Or, if

Inexpensive plastic

you'd rather not contribute to the local lab supply store, at least have a small pitcher and a measuring cup for each of your invitees (cheap plastic stuff from the dollar store works just fine).

Of course, you will need wine. Purchase 100% varietals of whatever wines appeal to you. If Bordeaux is your thing, pick up no less than a bottle of Cabernet Sauvignon, another of Merlot, and a third of Cabernet Franc, with Petit Verdot and/or Malbec also allowed. If your style is more Aussie or Washington state, try a blend of Shiraz and Cabernet Sauvignon, or if more Aussie and southern Rhone, consider Grenache, Syrah, and Mourvèdre, the classic GSM blend.

White combinations à la France might include Sauvignon Blanc with Sémillon; a northern Italian take would blend Chardonnay, Sauvignon (Blanc), Pinot Grigio, Pinot Bianco, Friulano and/or Gewürztraminer. Chardonnay-Sémillon blends are popular in Australia.

Rosé, rosé, rosé. Lest we forget the delicious possibilities in this category, especially when including the much-frowned-upon method of rosé production by blending red and white. Yet think of all the potential combinations: a base of neutral white wine like Ugni Blanc or Pinot Grigio or of a bolder white, say Verdejo, Gavi or Chardonnay, blended with a small percentage (note: too much red and the color and freshness of rosé will be lost) of Garnacha, Syrah, or whatever you like. Thousands of cuvées just waiting to be discovered!

Before diving in, though, sip the components, get a sense of the characteristics they do or do not bring to the table. The object is to create balance and harmony. For example, Merlot rounds out Cabernet Sauvignon, softening its tannins and creating a smoother, more approachable whole. In contrast, Sangiovese combined with Barbera is one high-acid wine with another; no benefit to be had from that partnership.

Pay attention to alcohol levels, tannins, mouthfeel, acidity, color, and residual sugar. Envision how one wine will "fit" into another. Try lots of blends but keep track of your trials. When you find a combination that sings, you want to be able to reproduce it. A good illustrative start would be to mix two parts of Cabernet

Sauvignon with one of Merlot. Taste it, try it, assess it. Then add in one part of Cabernet Franc. You now have a blend of 50% Cabernet Sauvignon, 25% Merlot, and 25% Cabernet Franc, a fairly standard left bank blend. How did each addition alter the cuvée? Which version did you prefer? Try changing the percentages or perhaps adding a small amount of Malbec or Petit Verdot.

Or you can start with a few test blends. Prepare a lineup of Chardonnay with 20% Sémillon, 40% Sémillon, 60% Sémillon, etc. Taste how they work together and how pleasing to your palate each combination is. When you zero in on your favorite, try adding a third wine and see how that affects the blend.

And since we aren't big on following the rules or the way it's always been done, turning your back on GSMs or Bordeaux blends completely can open some rather wacky doors. Why not experiment with grapes that have likely never even been introduced?

Tuscan stalwart Sangiovese, meet Agiorgitiko from the Nemea region of Greece. Saperavi of Georgia, may I present Pinot Noir, well-known in Burgundy (and elsewhere, I might add). Bobal, my old Spanish friend, have you met Dolcetto, from the Piemonte? And you, Pinotage, all the way from South Africa, allow me to introduce, from the lovely Loire valley, Cabernet Franc.

Ah, I see the others are still arriving. Sagrantino and Touriga Nacional and, look, there's Frappato and Syrah. And the whites, oh, excellent. Chardonnay, of course, and Grillo and Torrontés, and isn't that Godello and Pinot Bianco chatting in the back?

By this point, you and your blending buddies should be well on your way. Have fun, enjoy, taste each other's creations. Set a time limit for everyone to present his or her "premier cuvée" to the group as a whole. Taste through these final assemblages and vote on the winner. See who can create the most popular wine to accompany a particular food—which you will have on hand, of course. However you choose to proceed, this is one party where you can't help but learn more about wine. That, you gotta love. Cheers!

THIRTY-SEVEN
THIRTY-SEVEN

EMBRACE BOTH CORKS
AND SCREW CAPS

THERE'S A LOT OF NOISE IN THE WORLD OF WINE ABOUT the use of screw caps vs. corks as closures for wine bottles. Some stalwarts are surprisingly strident in their defense of tradition while others have little regard for the way it's always been done, for the familiar, for the ritual of pulling corks and presenting them for inspection.

As the controversy continues, albeit with less intensity than in years gone by, it behooves those less versed in this particular argument to understand what all the shouting is about. After all, if a wine lover takes sides or is asked his or her opinion, how much better to know, with some degree of certainty, what's being discussed.

Wine has a history of being stored and sealed in a variety of vessels that have evolved through the centuries. Early winemakers understood as clearly as we do the negative impact of exposure to air on a wine's smell, taste, and general soundness. The earliest closures, as we've discussed more than once, were likely patches of animal skin bound to the tops of jars or clay storage containers. With the advent of amphorae, narrow-necked and with a smaller opening, the job became easier. A twist of grasses or a whittled plug of wood stuck into the opening and covered by a thin slip of clay molded around the top or a smearing of pine resin to seal it against the air did a good job of preserving the contents.

Amphorae were the bottles of the ancient world and for three or four thousand years were used to store and transport wine, olives, olive oil, salt, even strips of meat and fish. The empties were disposed of much as we dispose of jars and bottles today: some were recycled, mainly broken up into small bits and mixed into concrete for construction projects, while most were smashed and tossed into a landfill. The famous Monte Testaccio, in Rome is, in fact, a hill that covers nearly a quarter million square feet while

A variety of amphorae

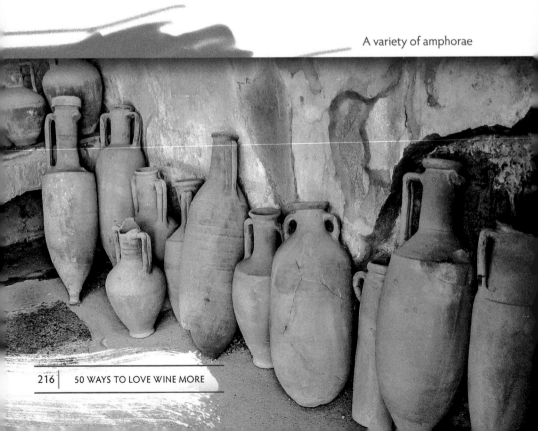

rising well over a hundred feet above the surrounding terrain—and is composed of centuries' worth of discarded, crushed amphorae, a large and early municipal dump.

By the first century AD, Rome had adopted the use of wooden barrels, introduced by the Gauls and Celts, for the transport of wine and other liquids. And so came the end of the era of amphorae, though smaller versions would still be used on a household level. Even into the early twentieth century, the well-to-do bought and stored wine by the barrel, drawing off by the jugful or pitcherful whatever amount was intended for that afternoon or evening's consumption.

Glass bottles, delicate and used for perfumes and unguents, had existed for millennia, but it was the advent of the coal-fired furnace in the seventeenth century that allowed for the production of stronger, thicker-walled uniform vessels. Even so, it wasn't until 1860, for instance, that wine in England could legally be sold in bottles and, hard though it may be to believe, it was only in 1979 that the United States approved of and adopted the 750 ml bottle as the standard measure for wine.

So as wine geeks bray and moan over the loss of cork or, alternately, over those who deride tradition, realize that the overwhelming majority of all the wine drinkers of history never once pulled a cork or poured wine from a glass bottle. Just a thought to keep it all in perspective.

Now, on to the recent past. Cork has an unbroken 150 year run as the wine bottle closure of choice. And it's done a damned good job. The seal is unusually good, the allowable transfer of oxygen seems to be about right, it is easily removed and reinserted, the supply is renewable, and the cost is low. But …

It seems a little fungus that goes by the handle TCA, full name 2,4,6-trichloroanisole, the child of naturally occurring fungi and the chlorophenol compounds found in pesticides and wood preservatives (remember, cork is a tree bark), likes to take up residence in the tiny cracks and crevices that, in essence, define a cork's structure.

And, unfortunately for oenophiles, it is entirely undetectable: it can be neither seen nor smelled nor even predicted. Until ...

Until inserted into a bottle of wine, when and where, for some not yet fully understood reason, it proceeds to foul both taste and smell. Though TCA presents no health hazard, it does irreparably ruin the wine it's supposed to protect. The effects of TCA contamination, referred to in wine as "corked" or "cork taint," are to infuse both the aroma and flavor of the wine with the smell and taste of wet dog or wet cardboard. In small doses it kills the freshness, the bright fruitiness of a wine and leaves behind a flat, unpleasant flavor; in higher concentrations it renders a wine clearly undrinkable, though in either case it should be returned to its place of purchase and disposed of down the drain of faulty wines.

"Yuk. No way I'm drinking this."

In the 1980s and 1990s there was a marked increase in the incidence of this scourge, to the point where drinkers were opening pricey aged bottles and equally pricey new releases only to be met by the distinctly unpleasant presence of a corked wine. It became a real problem. At one point, it was estimated that 10% of all cork-stoppered wines were rendered unpalatable by the presence of TCA.

The situation had become serious, affecting the economics of the entire industry. Cork producers were burning the midnight oil in laboratories and test cellars searching for a solution; meanwhile, wine lovers around the world witnessed the re-emergence of screw caps, aka Stelvin closures, from their past as the stopper of choice for low-end wines—i.e., pints of rotgut to jugs of who-knows-what— into a viable replacement for corks. Not to be outdone, other companies saw the opportunity and flooded the market with imitation corks and closures that quickly gained adherents.

There were synthetic corks made of plastic polymers, some extruded, some molded. Ersatz corks with a thin outer sleeve around what looked like minced bits of cork glued together. There were black ones and white ones; they came in green and purple and every color of the rainbow. Some slid out too easily; others stuck in the neck of a bottle and could be removed only with a stout corkscrew and a strong pair of hands. But it was the passage of oxygen that was their undoing. The synthetics let in far too much O_2 and were soon relegated to the minors.

Screw caps, on the other hand, were eating away at cork's previous dominance. New Zealand, in particular, turned its back on corks, with more than 90% of its wineries switching to screw caps; in Australia there was a nearly 80% conversion. Screw caps were gaining ground, especially for soon-to-be-drunk white wines and less expensive reds.

Meanwhile, cork producers were making progress, improving sanitation and working on methods of mass inoculation of batches of corks to eliminate any TCA. At the same time, numerous studies showed that screwcaps allowed too little oxygen to pass into the bottle, resulting in reductive notes of sulfur and burnt rubber.

And so the winds shift yet again. We have now reached the point where the good folks in Portugal and Spain (source of about 80% of the world cork supply) have come close to completely eliminating the TCA taint problem. This is very good news for winemakers producing age-worthy wines and for the retailers and distributors who sell them. It's also a development of great comfort to wine drinkers who find reassurance and satisfaction in the ritual of removing a cork and slowly twisting it off the corkscrew while chatting with fellow geeks about the wine they're preparing to share.

The screw cap manufacturers have likewise made progress in improving their product, experimenting with various liners to find one that allows the right amount of oxygen to permeate the cap. No doubt, it's been somewhat of a learning curve for sommeliers to forsake the choreography of pulling and presenting, with panache, the cork from a bottle of wine for the customer's inspection. But life goes on; screwcaps are discreetly pocketed and the wine is gaily poured.

To be honest, it's nice at times to pull an everyday white or red from the cooler and quickly snap off its cap. It's hard to complain about an effective closure that requires no tools. Still, most consumers in the United States and other wine-consuming nations continue to prefer cork, and associate it with romance, tradition, and quality. Unless you're in the closure business, it's hard not to think this debate has run its course. And rather than argue about one vs. the other, I'd much rather you pour something delicious into my glass and be done with it. *Saúde!*

THIRTY-EIGHT
THIRTY-EIGHT

PEEL BACK THE MYSTERY
OF ORANGE WINES

Y ES, THEY DO MAKE ORANGE WINE IN FLORIDA, AND MANGO
wine and grapefruit wine and even key lime wine. But it's
not the fruit being discussed here; rather, it's the color, as in
rosé. In fact, you may have noticed in the past few years some additions to wine lists labeled as "orange wines." What's being referred
to here are white wines left to macerate on their skins, just as red
wines are, to absorb the polyphenols, the flavonoids and anthocyanins that skin contact imparts to the must.

As rosé wines are produced by whisking the grape juice, pre-
fermentation, quickly off the red grape skins so that too much color
doesn't leech into the juice (or must), orange wines are produced by
leaving the white grapes—skins, seeds, and all—with the pulp and
juice to stew together, so the must picks up as much color, tannins,

Orange wines of different white grapes

etc. as possible from the white skins. It's obvious that white grape skins don't contain as much color or other phenolics as do reds, but nonetheless they are still able to contribute noticeable color, texture, tannins, and complexity to the resulting "white" wine, now more ruddy, coppery, or orange in color. Voilà, orange wine. The "new" category that completes the circle.

Crushed red grapes macerated on their skins equals red wine; crushed red grape juice poured off the skins equals rosé wine. Crushed white grapes macerated on their skins equals orange wine; crushed white grape juice poured off the skins equals white wines. So, in fact, the reintroduction to the world of orange wine simply balances the scales.

In examining ancient winemaking techniques and facilities, we find clear evidence of both approaches. It was common practice to crush or stomp grapes, usually by foot, and let the juice flow immediately into larger fermentation vessels with little or no maceration. It was also common to fill a large container with grapes, crush them enough to begin fermentation, and leave the entire batch to soak and ferment together. Local custom, and perhaps whom you learned from, was apparently the determining factor, with some regions favoring the former approach and others favoring the latter.

Regardless of the particulars of ancient winemaking, in more recent times the approach has been to macerate reds on their skins for as long as possible, extracting the maximum color, texture, and phenolic input. There seems to be an unwritten consensus that deeper color equates to a richer, more "profound" wine. On the white side, things have been just the opposite; consumers and winemakers both have gravitated to clean, clear, highly filtered and fined "brilliant" or "star bright" wines as being indicative of

Winemaking facility in Crete, circa 3500 BC

White grapes macerating in Georgian *kvevri*

white wine quality. Why light reds or orange whites have been out of favor is hard to say exactly.

Fortunately, all that is changing. The preference pendulum has swung back to flavor as opposed to extraction alone. Lovers of old Burgundies, for example, wines often pale in color but riotous on the palate, will be pleased by this recent evolution in appreciation. As will those who enjoy white wines but have often found that even the best of them are too often stripped of character, reduced to one-note wonders.

Orange wines are the whites you always wished for. Wines with the complexity and mouthfeel of well-made reds, wines that go better with food, wines that insist on capturing your attention.

A few days, a week, maybe two, a month, or more, and those less intense white grape skins, seeds, and stems give so much oomph, so much individuality to a wine. They transmit the terroir, the soil type and climate, and peculiarities of the vintage so much more effectively than their heavily fined and filtered cousins. How can you expect to know a wine's place, its surroundings, its potential, if you won't allow it the chance to be more than clarified grape juice?

Orange wines, for all the reasons mentioned, are a growing, if still small and unfamiliar category. A quick look around the vinous landscape shows more and more mainstream wineries releasing a "skin-contact" or "skin-fermented" Chardonnay, Ribolla Gialla, Sauvignon Blanc, or what have you. And with such influential wineries paying attention, the trend to orange could certainly accelerate.

Many of the winemakers who initiated this approach to white winemaking—led by the adventurous Josko Gravner, from the Friuli region of northeast Italy—did so as a reaction to over-manipulation: the chemical additives, the stabilizers and color concentrates that are too widely accepted in the production of modern wines. They are proponents of so-called "natural wine," believers that less is more, that wines made without pesticides in the vineyards or additions of sulfur or even aging in new oak allows for a truer, a purer wine.

As with many heartfelt movements, a certain percentage of early advocates came perilously close to tossing out the goodies with the grape juice. The first experiments were not uniformly successful. Oxidized and faulty wines, made using none of the benefits of contemporary winemaking, were often hard to drink, harder still to enjoy. One could pick through a lineup of orange wines, the few being made at the end of the 1990s and early 2000s, and have serious doubts about a good number of them.

Fortunately, winemakers on both sides of the debate have improved their methods and come closer together in their philosophies. The good news for votaries of the holy juice is that deliciousness has reentered the equation. Gorgeous orange wines, from regions as disparate as Savoie, Slovenia, South Africa, Margaret River, Sonoma and even Long Island are increasingly available.

These are wines worth trying. Beautifully colored, with texture, tannins, and complexity that wine lovers aren't used to in white wines, they provide an alternative, an especially food-friendly alternative, to the clean, clear, and crisp whites that will continue to find a place in our cellars and our vinous hearts. There is, after all, room for red, white, orange, rosé, sparkling, still, sweet, *and* dry in our panoply of oenological delights. Find them, try them, enjoy them. Here, here!

THIRTY-NINE

THIRTY-NINE

EXPAND YOUR VARIETAL FAMILIARITY

PERUSE THE MAJORITY OF WINE LISTS AND YOU ARE PRESENTED with the same twenty or thirty grapes. The white side offers Pinot Grigio, Pinot Bianco (perhaps), Albariño, Sauvignon Blanc, Chardonnay, Chenin Blanc, Garganega (Soave), Cortese (Gavi), Riesling, Torrontés (now and again), Verdejo, Vermentino, Grüner Veltliner, Gewürztraminer, and maybe Viognier. Reds on display might include Pinot Noir, Cabernet Sauvignon, Cabernet Franc, Merlot, Syrah, Barbera, Tempranillo (Rioja, Toro, and more), Sangiovese (Chianti, Brunello), Grenache, Montepulciano, Nero d'Avola, Malbec, Nebbiolo (Barolo, Barbaresco), and Zinfandel. Perhaps a sprinkling more or less.

Sure, one can find more extensive lists and lists that focus on select regions or wine types, and it is true that a Sauvignon Blanc from the Loire Valley is quite distinct from one produced on the South Island of New Zealand, but when you consider that well over a thousand grape varieties are made into wine in commercial quantities, it's apparent that what most of us are regularly exposed to is but a narrow slice of *Vitis vinifera*.

While the wines that are routinely encountered may be very good and we may have developed a penchant for their flavors and aromas, there's an awfully big world of other juice out there, one that can be fascinating to study and taste, and perhaps add to your growing collection.

Getting to know other members of the wine grape family is not unlike exploring the universe. Consider the widely planted, most commonly bought and sold varieties (those making up the bulk of wine lists and retail shelf facings) as the sun of this system, the center, at least of our corner of the universe. Around these, at increasing distances, revolve other, though still familiar names: Dolcetto, Sémillon, Carménère, Arneis, Aglianico, Fiano, Grillo, Carignan, Mourvèdre, Moschofilero, Negroamaro, Nerello Mascalese, Müller-Thurgau, Trebbiano, Pedro Ximénez, Petite Sirah, Melon de Bourgogne.

All these can still be found on *someone's* wine list, *somewhere*. But not often enough. And many would please you greatly if you're not yet versed in their vinous wonders. The reality is that grapes that grow easily in varied terroirs are and always have been more widely disseminated around the globe. Just kinda makes sense. And historically, wines produced near routes of trade and transportation—rivers and waterways, for the most part, and railroads more recently—have a greater likelihood of being exported to other cities and countries where they're exposed to new consumers, boosting their demand.

But fads in food and drink, as in everything else, come and go. Empires crumble, centers of influence shift, weather patterns favorable to viticulture wax and wane, and a grape or a wine that was wildly popular in some part of the world falls out of favor and is relegated to the backwaters of a no-longer important region.

This cycle has recurred time and again in the history of wine. Of the most favored ancient varieties, we know little. Wines lauded by the royal hosts of Babylon, or served and enjoyed by the Pharaohs of Egypt, or described by Pliny or Virgil as the best of their day have vanished in the winds of time. More recently, we do know of the past popularity of Tokaji, sweet nectar of a wine made from the Furmint grape, in eighteenth- and nineteenth-century Europe. Lost to the subjugation of Hungary by the Soviet Union, Tokaji and Furmint, in both sweet and dry versions, are only now reemerging onto the world wine scene. And Edgar Allan Poe's story "The Cask of Amontillado," published in 1846, gives us an insight into the popularity of Amontillado, and Sherries in general, not so long ago. Clearly, these are wines that too few enthusiasts enjoy these days.

Fortunately, a wine much appreciated and even granted special tax status by King Henry III of England, a favorite of Pope John Paul XXII in the 1300s, beloved by Peter the Great in the late 1600s, and main component in the wines of Bordeaux through the seventeenth and eighteenth centuries can still, thanks to the winegrowers of Argentina and a gritty young group of vignerons in southwestern France, be enjoyed under the varietal name Malbec.

So as you explore the next "orbit" of grapes, of Assyrtiko and Falanghina, Greco di Tufo, Grenache Blanc and Ribolla Gialla, Sagrantino, Touriga Nacional, and Xinomavro consider the place these varieties have had, and continue to have, among local wine lovers in their home regions. It is said that Italy alone produces some quantity of eight hundred or more different wines; Greece, the home of Dionysius, on the order of two or three hundred.

The gods of wine may offer much, but it's up to us to accept. Neither Bacchus nor his Greek precursor, the aforementioned Dionysius, ever directed followers to restrict themselves to a mere handful of varieties. They were both, in fact, rather well-known adherents of plenty—in all things—especially those involving wine and celebration. In their honor, in recognition of the bounty of grape types with which they have endowed the world, it is only right to expand and explore, to search and to sample, to show these long-lived gods of plenty our thanks and appreciation by consuming, with gusto, what they have laid before us.

Don't be stuck in a vinous rut. Fly your palate to the more distant circumambulations of Baga, Blaufränkisch, and Alicante Bouschet, of Picpoul and Erbaluce and Timorasso. Of Listán Negro and Gaglioppo; of Teroldego, Tinta Barroca, and Plavac Mali; Chasselas, Petit Manseng, Hondarrabi Zuri, and Malagousia. You have, no doubt, figured out by now that the list could go on for pages. Our planet is awash in wines, most of which the average wine lover has yet to taste.

As strange or foreign as any of the above-named grapes may seem, they are all available, duly fermented and bottled, in stores around the globe. Most are wines that any connoisseur, bon vivant, or habitué would take pleasure in serving to his or her most discerning associates. Use the wonders of the e-sources at your fingertips to learn about them: each has a unique place in the world of wine, and many are compelling stories in and of themselves. And then buy. And drink.

Grapes to the left of me and grapes to the right. Here I am, stuck in the middle, trying as many as I can, hopefully with you!

FORTY

FORTY

TAKE SOME CLASSES; FIND A SEMINAR

S UGGESTING THAT READERS TAKE A WINE CLASS IS NOT done lightly. As with most classes or educational experiences, some are good, some are great, and some are best avoided. And yet the good ones offer so much to the nascent aficionado that it would be remiss to ignore the opportunity.

Wine classes exist in all sorts of venues, sponsored by various interests, associations, and organizations. Some are intended simply to make money, others to sell or represent a particular retailer, "family" of wine, or wine-related products. With a little searching, you will find them at wine shops, liquor stores, restaurants, cooking schools, wine schools, community colleges, and even online.

What is most important, though, isn't the "where" or the "what" but rather the "who." Who's teaching, that is. The good news for students is that wine, by its very nature, breeds almost ridiculous levels of enthusiasm. Combine that with some hard-earned knowledge and years of experience and the result is quite likely an instructor bursting with enthusiasm who looks forward to every class and every opportunity to enlighten the world just a bit more about the fascinating topic of wine: its history, production, styles, regions, vintages, and varieties.

Welcome to wine class.

While excellent and inexpensive classes can be found at many of the aforementioned locales, another suggestion is to avail yourself of the leading credentialing bodies, well-known and highly regarded throughout the wine community, that not only certify the industry's top professionals but also provide classes and courses to the wine-interested public. These include the Court of Master Sommeliers, the Wine and Spirits Education Trust, the Society of Wine Educators, the Wine Scholar Guild, and the International Wine Guild.

The benefit of taking courses or classes sponsored or provided by these organizations is that you are assured of accurate, up-to-date information presented by instructors who know and love wine, and whose passion shows through at every step. It's fun learning from someone who cares and enjoys being there as much as you do. These groups are easily found online and usually post schedules and locations for their various classes and other wine-oriented events. And should you be pressed for time or located where few actual classes are available, most also offer online instruction, including a variety of webinars.

Another incredible opportunity that too few wine lovers take advantage of is attending seminars. What's exciting about seminars is that attendees often have a chance to taste ultra-premium wines, wines that are otherwise impossible to find—or too expensive to buy. You like Pinot Noir? How about a lineup featuring half a dozen outstanding Burgundies contrasted with a selection of the best Pinots from Oregon or Central Otago? Or maybe first-growth Bordeaux from different vintages. Or, for you Italian fans, eight or ten Amarones dating back to the 1980s. Sure, these events aren't free, but the price of admission is a generally a fraction of what even a single bottle would cost.

Most wine fairs and festivals offer seminars as part of their program, and unlike trade tastings, where you have to actually work in the wine industry to attend, these seminars are open to anyone with an interest in the topic who registers and shows up. Again, check the websites and promotional materials of any wine fairs or wine and food festivals being held in your area.

Classes and seminars are also perfect to get your wine buddies involved in. Imagine you and a friend who loves dessert wine at a

Wine seminars are fun, educational, and a great value.

Sauternes tasting: 1967, 1975, 1976, 1983, 1990, 1997, 2001, 2003, 2009. Historic vintages, one knockout wine after another. Just the kind of tasting one can indulge in on the "seminar circuit" that would be literally impossible to experience on your own. Don't overlook this source of both wine knowledge and world-class tastings that will provide you not only with a happy palate but also with wine memories to last a lifetime. Come now, what's not to love?

FORTY-ONE

FORTY-ONE

DRINK WITH FOREIGNERS

"THERE'S A POINT TO THIS?" YOU ASK. IT'S AN ODD suggestion, one might concede, but yes, there are absolutely, without question, a whole slew of reasons to imbibe with folks from other lands: they have a different perspective, different expectations, even a different vocabulary when it comes to wine. If we interact with or get feedback only from people with the same outlook and assumptions as our own, it is difficult to expand our vision or develop a more complete understanding of the place wine holds in our world.

Different nations are home to different foods, different fruits and vegetables, different preparations, and, consequently, different palates. Be it a predilection (or revulsion) for sweet, sour, bitter, salty, umami, fatty, fishy, fermented, fried, boiled, baked, bloody, raw, rancid, rustic, squishy, squirmy, soft or smooth, silky, slimy, or highly odoriferous, their approach to and appreciation of wine is more than possibly distinct from our own. Assuming by definition there are no absolute rights or wrongs in the matter of taste, this alone should make it at least interesting, if not enlightening, to sip and savor and discuss the good and the not so wonderful with those weaned on the milk of a different mother.

Great moments with occasional flashes of insight can be had by conversing with drinkers from other cultures about wine in general or any given wine in particular. On *their* home turf, your flavor prejudice should be readily noticeable, though this isn't the actual point. Better than wasting time or energy worrying about the contrast in palates is to give some thought as to how environment and expectation affect one's response. And if, by exploring others' preferences, you can enlarge your own spectrum of pleasure, the exercise will have been a success.

Think back to your first sip of beer, your first taste of wine, your first carrot or stalk of broccoli. Among the "firsts" there are surely things that still repel you, but among those you weren't hard-wired to reject are others that put you off due more to lack of familiarity. Once you tried those carrots a few times or had your second or third, or fifth or tenth, sip of wine, it all started to taste quite delicious. Which doesn't mean you're going to give up your Montrachet for baby mouse wine (yes, there is such a thing, and yes, it is what it sounds like), but it does mean other organoleptic orientations may be worthy of consideration.

The clear divergence in wine tastes and preferences between Brits and Americans being a case in point, one need only consider their fondness for the well- to very well-aged—the British palate—vs. the American bent toward up-front fruit and a fuller body. Surely these populations are as similar as any two can be, yet the marked disparity in their palates should be instructive for enthusiasts on both sides of the pond.

After all, subjects of the crown were responsible for Port, for Madeira, and for keeping Bordeaux in business through more than one lean period in history. They have clearly been drinking for much longer than we Yanks, and if we pay a bit of attention to their druthers, the worst that can happen is that we'll enjoy more wine marked by age, maturity, and added complexity (thanks to the tertiary characteristics that evolve as the sugars, acids, alcohols, and polyphenols link and unlink, creating new flavors and aromas: truffles and black olive, for example) and take a second look at those magnificent fortified wines, Port and Madeira, so appreciated in days gone by, that "modern" wine drinkers seem to overlook.

For our British cousins, enjoying a glass of fermented fruit juice (i.e., a New World wine) that still has some actual fruit presence to it can't be such a bad thing. And with all that drizzly weather the United Kingdom is known for, a dry table wine whose body and alcohol levels approach that of your beloved Port should be welcome, at least on occasion, rather than off-putting. We really do have much in common, as we both have excellent and valid points to make about what we find desirable in a good glass of vino.

Wine travel being the pleasure it is, how cool to sip and swap perspectives with an Italian dissecting Chianti in Tuscany, a Spaniard holding forth on Tempranillo in Rioja, an Argentinean reacting to Malbec in Mendoza, or a Kiwi sipping Chardonnay in Hawke's Bay. And fortunately, drinking with foreigners is easily pursued, with equal benefit, wherever you live or travel.

One can, while sharing a bottle in Washington, D.C., exchange descriptors and their meanings with Chinese enthusiasts who use such terms as *yangmei* and *dried hawthorn, ginkgo nut* and *pandan leaf.* Or with French aficionados, declaring their preference for lower alcohol while hammering at the importance of terroir at wine bars in New York City; Germans in Miami who love vibrant, dry whites with what we consider to be red-wine food; Armenians in L.A. or Chileans in Houston or Slovakians in Minneapolis. It's not the where; it's the what-are-they-saying-and-why-do-they-believe-it that demands attention. A good tête-á-tête over a bottle of Syrah next to one of Sake with a taster from Tokyo on a visit to San Francisco can be downright illuminating.

Ah, the great big, sprawling, silly, sloppy, ancient, aromatic, wonderful world of wine. Enjoy it. Find someone from somewhere else and buy him or her a glass of the best wine in the house. Then listen more than you speak; ask more than you answer. This wine thing—you gotta love it. *Kanpai*!

FORTY-TWO

F O R T Y - T W O

TAKE ADVANTAGE OF THE WORLD'S GREAT WINE BARGAINS

I N THIS ERA OF ESCALATING PRICES AND WINES THAT ARE bought and sold for hundreds of dollars per bottle, who among us hasn't occasionally felt the shadow of despair flit across our vinous hearts? Perhaps you've read a glowing review or pulled a prized bottle from the top shelf of your nearby wine shop only to be stopped short by the price.

"It sounds fabulous," you think, "but who's going to pay a week's salary for a bottle of wine?"

Who, indeed? Yet the financially moderate to middle to even well-off habitué often runs headlong into the brick wall of ridiculous pricing. "I'd like to sample those trophy wines as much as the next grape nut," you say. Unfortunately, minus the intervention of a fairy godmother, that's unlikely to happen. So, what to do? Cry and bemoan your dearth of stupid money? Throw yourself at the you're-never-going-to-find-it mercy of the hapless retailer? Don mask and pistol and abscond with the goods?

Interesting, semi-normal responses, but with little chance of success. So instead, drink with people known for their cellars, attend those aforementioned seminars and conferences (refer to Chapter Forty), or pool resources with friends who would like a taste of the same rarity as yourself. These strategies will all put a glass of something breathtaking in front of you now and again. But for everyday pleasure, few of us can afford to overlook the thousands of good to great wines to be had for a most reasonable levy.

Yet even beyond (or below) that lies a cache of wines quite delightful that continue to fly under the radar of too many devotees of the good stuff. These wines are well-made, perhaps forgotten or simply overlooked or dismissed by aspiring wine snobs (yes, such people do exist) more concerned with creating outward impressions than communing with the grapes of rapture. So ignore what the swells are drinking tonight and mine the incredible bargains yet extant sprinkled here and there around the globe.

Let us consider first that lovely, lithe, food-friendly Iberian, the simple yet remarkably tasty white known far and wide as Vinho Verde—green wine—not for its color but for its youth and exuberance. With a bowl of clams and broth and chorizo on a warm summer's eve there is nothing better; no overpriced Montrachet, no Blanc de blanc Champagne, no Gewürztraminer or Pinot Gris comes close to the perfection of a spritzy, sassy ten-dollar quaff from the northern hinterlands of Portugal. With green salads, with sushi, with a picnic by the beach or tuna salad sandwich in hand, this is truly one of the world's great wine bargains. You can, with effort, find one that's not ridiculously inexpensive, but why bother? This wine is both straightforward and complex, fermented and bottled young, dry but with a touch of spritz to add to its character. There is nothing difficult here, yet even the most sophisticated wine lovers will gratefully appreciate this party going, have-another-glass incarnation of goodness. And please, choose the low-priced option—as most of them are—and treat yourself and your wine friends to a genuine glass of pleasure.

Another satisfying white to consider isn't the product of any particular region or appellation and is certainly available in pricier versions. But the Sauvignon Blanc grape, by its very nature, tends to maintain its varietal "typicity," or characteristic, regardless of factors that may greatly affect other wines. Many who enjoy and appreciate Sauvignon Blanc prize the lemony, grapefruit, cut-grass, green pepper flavors and aromas for which the variety is so well-known.

Fortunately for the folks who savor this wine, be it with fish, shrimp, shellfish, asparagus, salads or goat cheese, or as an aperitif or just to relax by the pool, Sauvignon Blanc maintains its green, citrusy, herbaceous qualities whether it's grown with tender loving care or not, meaning the least expensive bottlings of this wine can be surprisingly good and to many wine lovers are barely distinguishable from the most costly Sauvignon Blancs on the market.

Whether from Chile, New Zealand, California (at times called Fumé Blanc), Canada, France (those labeled Sancerre or Pouilly-Fumé will be at the top of the price list), Australia, or South Africa, you can count on a very good bottle of Sauvignon Blanc for a surprisingly modest outlay. Overcropping, lack of canopy management, and picking too early—all sins of the mega-producers who pump out a million or two bottles every vintage—have little effect on this grape or the wines it produces. So grab that ten-dollar bottle, throw some shrimp on the barbie, and have a delicious dinner with a wine accompaniment that consistently over-delivers.

We have looked so far at two solid bargains in the category of white wine; shall we try two sparklers that most everyone enjoys and that clearly cost less than they should? Bubblies are always a good choice because they make folks smile, that alone being reason enough to drink them as part of your regular "rotation." But if there's

Enjoying the spoils of smart shopping

a promotion at work, someone has just announced an engagement (you?), a friend is visiting from out of town, or you're just happy to be alive, reward yourself with a celebratory toast of something that'll make you feel good all the way down.

First up, as you may have guessed, is that suave Italian, sweet and sexy, or dry and delightful, the toast of Venice, offspring of the Glera grape and known to all the world as Prosecco. Most versions are fizzy and easygoing, a great match with food—Venetians drink it with everything—and it comes in both dry and slightly sweeter styles, which allows it to please a variety of palates. Prosecco is probably the consistently best-quality, low-priced sparkling wine on the market.

A step (make that half a step) up in price but still delivering a cost-to-quality ratio that makes even a tightwad chuckle is Cava, made in Spain via the same process responsible for Champagne, though using the Spanish grapes Macabeo, Parellada, and Xarel-lo, and these days maybe a touch of Chardonnay. A good Cava—and there are many—is truly a great bargain. For those on a tight budget or anyone interested in serious savings, this is as close to Champagne as it gets. Lively, bubbly, fun, tasty, especially good with salty foods from mixed nuts to caviar and a wonderful welcome to friends or family visiting your gracious abode, this one belongs at the top of your shopping list.

And now, an entire category: rosés. These wines are such a great deal, on multiple levels, that no one dares talk about it, as if everyone else will suddenly see the value and start buying them up by the case. Well, news flash: the stampede has begun and the cases are already flying. Yet prices continue to dwell in the amazing department. Stop by an end-cap or floor display of rosés in the spring or early summer and you'll feel like you're in a discount store: incredible selection, unbelievable prices.

But believe them. Where else can you buy such satisfying warm-weather quaffing from France, Italy, Spain, the United States, South America, or just about any other region using every conceivable wine grape or combination thereof for the price of a bar of soap (okay, two maybe, the good stuff, those handmade bars)?

One wino's first rosé may have been drunk in a moment of ecstasy while vacationing on the shores of the Mediterranean, another's while sitting around the leaky aboveground pool in Uncle Billy's backyard watching kids doing belly flops with some weenies burning on the rusty three-legged grill nearby. It's not important. Few things go so well with a sunny day and a moment to relax as a glass of chilled rosé. And what a steal!

Which leaves only the reds. You think reds are going to be a problem, don't you? Ha, ha! Not at all. And we're talking good quality here. It's not a bargain if it's lousy; it's a deal only if it's very good and costs less than it's worth.

That being the case, let's head to the Rhone Valley of southern France, the home of such famed appellations as Hermitage, Côte Rôtie, and Châteauneuf-du-Pape. In fact, this wine-heavy region has five red wine appellations in its northern sector and more than a dozen in the much larger southern Rhone. All the vineyards not

included in these more renowned locales together form the Côtes du Rhone (meaning hills or slopes of the Rhone), their own noncontiguous appellation that stretches over a hundred miles from north to south.

The wines we're seeking, labeled either Côtes du Rhone or Côtes du Rhone Village, are typically blends of Grenache, Syrah, Mourvèdre, Cinsault, and/or Carignan. While they may not have the power or focus of the top appellations of the Rhone region, they are serious, well-made, rich, and full-bodied examples of Old World winemaking. Not to mention that their cost is but a fraction of what's charged for wines produced, in many cases, from vineyards just down the road. These are not light, fruity, frivolous wines, but they are among the world's great wine values.

Next and last on our list of bargains too good to pass up are the hundreds of high-quality French wines with the designation *Bordeaux Supérieur*. Bordeaux is the largest region in France and perhaps the most important wine region in the world. This gigantic patchwork of vineyards straddles two rivers and covers close to three hundred thousand acres (about 125,000 hectares). It contains sixty-plus appellations and churns out nine hundred million bottles of wine every year.

Wine geeks are familiar with the top names, the so-called classified growths. Châteaux Lafite, Latour, Margaux, Mouton, Haut-Brion, and their right bank counterparts Pétrus, Angélus, Ausone, Pavie, Cheval Blanc. And following them, another hundred and fifty or so, depending on who's doing the counting. These are universally considered among the finest wines in the world, the peak of viniculture and viticulture combined. Focused, powerful, elegant, and age-worthy, the ultimate expression of grapes into wine.

Yet in that sea of nine hundred million bottles, this top tier, the very expensive product of these glorious, prestigious châteaux, account for less than five percent of the region's total output. There are not a hundred and fifty or two hundred or even a thousand producers to thank for Bordeaux's amazing abundance. The real number is more than seven thousand. Most "châteaux," however, are modest workaday wineries, family-run, that strive to create the best wine they can in a region blessed with wine-friendly soils and occasionally wine-friendly weather.

A significant chunk of this product is sourced from vineyards located among and adjacent to those of the big names. Oak-aged for at least a year and adhering to minimum alcohol levels, these blends of Merlot, Cabernet Sauvignon, Cabernet Franc, and possibly a dash of Petit Verdot, Malbec, or Carménère are allowed to wear the label *Bordeaux Supérieur* because they are just that: superior to most wines of Bordeaux.

Which, combined with their exceptionally modest price tags, makes them a helluva deal for anyone with a taste for structured, earthy, tannic expressions of Merlot, Cabernet, et al. To enhance your odds of scoring big while spending little, look for the phrase "Mis en Bouteille au Château" or "Mis en Bouteille a la Propriete" printed on the label. This will ensure that you're buying a wine made and bottled by a winemaker at the winery and not grown and vinified by one person and then sold to another in bulk to blend and bottle as he or she sees fit. It's also a good idea, as Bordeaux is a region that varies greatly from one vintage to the next, to select your Bordeaux Supérieur from the strongest years. There are vintage charts aplenty, whether online or in wine publications, to consult as to the best of recent years.

So, in the great big world of pricey wines, these are the budget bottles, the vinous discount store, if you will, that's open to all of us. High-quality juice, cut-rate prices. What better combo? Plus, since these are wines with significant international distribution, chances are good that you can shop for them wherever you're located.

Vinho Verde: easy-drinking, food friendly, a great quencher that makes no pretense. Sauvignon Blanc: flush with personality, distinct and delicious, a lover of fish, shrimp, chicken, Asian, even asparagus. Prosecco and Cava: soft and fizzy or bold and bubbly, smilin' wines, whatever the reason, whatever the season, they make you want another bottle. Rosé: one of just a handful of non-profound wines that speaks to its drinkers, loves summer, loves sunny days by the sea, loves you—really, the last time I enjoyed a bottle, it told me so. And it goes with everything. Côtes du Rhone: fruity, spicy, structured, mid-weight, good alcohol, mouthwatering. Bordeaux Supérieur: terroir, tannins, structure, berry, cherry, plums and earthiness galore, enjoys the table, meats and cheeses.

For your pleasure, fellow budgeteers, a rainbow of whites, sparklers, reds and rosés, a perfect choice whatever the occasion. Yes, there are others that could have been included, but perhaps you will enjoy these so much that you will seek out additional deals and share them with your own circle of friends. After all, isn't that what wine is all about?

FORTY-THREE
FORTY-THREE

FOR THE LOVE OF CHOCOLATE

I T IS REASONABLE TO ASSUME THAT WINE AND CHOCOLATE made each other's acquaintance some five hundred years ago, most likely in the verdant hallways of ancient Mexico, and have maintained a skeptical, one might even say love-hate relationship ever since. After all, from their earliest days, one as the favored beverage of the conquerors, the other of the conquered, these delicious libations have spent much of their time in competition.

Think of it: chocolate, or *xocoatl*, as the Aztecs called it, was a brewed, frothy drink of sacred origin, worthy of ritual inclusion in the holiest of ceremonies. The gods themselves, it was believed, had bled upon the pods of cacao to endow them with hallowed presence. Compare this with wine, likewise a drink of divinity, stand-in for the blood of Christ, and so highly regarded that vines brought with them from Spain were planted in the very first settlements of the conquistadors. And just as clerics of the holy Catholic church celebrated the

Eucharist with raised chalices of wine, so too did servants of the omnipotent court of the Aztecs offer to their sacred emperor, Montezuma, finely wrought cups of gold, filled with serving after serving of reverently frothed chocolate.

One can only speculate as to how many humans, at that time and in that place, were able to try both and make whatever comparisons they would. This parallel track continued, however, as wine became more widespread in the New World and cacao beans were shipped back to Europe for the next three hundred years. It wasn't until the mid-1800s that chocolate became available in solid form. For the first time, instead of choosing to drink wine or drink chocolate, one could have them together: a wine to sip, a chocolate to nibble. And at that point, the two embarked on a new phase in their relationship.

Chocolate, (dark, unprocessed especially) born of the gods, delightful to the taste, said to endow good health in small doses and to trigger feel-good transmissions of endorphins, serotonin, and dopamine, has entwined itself with the culture

of wine, likewise a gift of the gods, a pleasure to the palate, said to promote good health in small amounts and also to stimulate our production of endorphins, serotonin, and dopamine. How remarkable that these two plants, one a small evergreen tree, *Theobroma cacao*, and the other a climbing woodland vine, *Vitis vinifera*, should be so complementary, in taste as well as in effect.

And so, let us turn to taste. The beauty of wine-and-chocolate pairing is that there are no rules. Not even an underpinning of "white wine with fish, red wine with meat." Nothing. No way and no one to say what's right or wrong. How refreshing! It is all, and only, about each individual's palate. Some like their wine sweet, some like it dry. Some like chocolate pure and dark, others prefer it with added sugar or filled with cherries or crèmes or mousse. Just as the Aztecs were fond of flavoring their frothy brew with maize, vanilla, aromatic flowers, herbs, honey, or chili pepper, today's chocolate makers offer versions with ginger, coconut, curry powder, sea salt, chili, bacon, and much else. Chocolate is about pleasure; if it tickles your happy spot, what else need be said?

The accompanying wine should do just the same, and the options are many. A dark, bitter high-quality chocolate is an almost savory experience and coats the mouth with a delicious essence that plays beautifully with Cabernet Sauvignon? Merlot? Malbec? Shiraz? Amarone? Unless you prefer something sweet to counter the bitterness, in which case you may want to audition a Vintage Port or an LBV Port. A Rutherglen Muscat might be the cat's meow, or a Vin Santo or PX Sherry or a late-harvest Zinfandel.

Not everyone is enamored of high-percentage, unsweetened cacao. Some folks would rather pop a luscious, creamy chunk of milk chocolate, perfectly sweetened, into their greedy maw. Following which, a healthy sip of Banyuls or Cream Sherry or Tawny Port, perhaps Prosecco or Sauternes or Tokaji would be the perfect choice. As stated, there is no right or wrong. Should you require further proof of that premise, simply look online for wine-and-chocolate pairings. Read half a dozen of the top ten results and try to keep from chuckling. Expert A will declare that dry wine should be paired only with "this" type of chocolate and never with "that." Expert B will pontificate on the glories of sweet wine, and sweet wine only, with any type of chocolate, while Expert C will insist that dry wines should be matched only with "that" and never with "this." All from credentialed, experienced know-nothings who refuse to accept the preeminence of your palate over theirs. In other words, one says "up," the other says "down," and they both claim to be right.

So, moving along, more chocolate than not is neither pure dark nor straight milk. Most falls into that category of flavored and formed bars, cakes, and candies. Blend in the already mentioned chilies, cherries, etc. and augment that with orange, coffee, caramel, buttercream, almonds, mint, lavender, hazelnuts, nougat, and, just for fun, *dulce de leche* or wasabi. Wow! What a wild crazy run our old friend *Theobroma cacao* is on these days.

Regardless of the possibilities, you and your sweetie are going to need a perfect wine match, or many, to go with all this absurdly scrumptious chocolate. The best approach—admittedly requiring a bit of time and commitment on your part (by the way, have Champagne and Ice Wine been mentioned?)—is to settle in for a relaxed evening of tasting and testing. Your favorite four or six chocolate indulgences and an ecumenical mix of broad-shouldered reds, slightly sweet bubbles, and full-on dessert wines.

Close your eyes, pop a taste of something *xocoatl*-based into your mouth, and chew and savor very slowly. It's amazing how wine suggestions will start to run through your brain. Select and sip. Repeat. Again. And yet again. Ah, the satisfaction. Love it.

FORTY-FOUR
FORTY FOUR

TRAIN YOUR TASTER
(GET HARD-CORE)

FORTY-FOUR CHAPTERS IN, IT MIGHT BE TIME TO ADMIT that your interest in the glories of grape juice (of the fermented variety, that is) exceeds the cursory. Which is something to be proud of. And if you have read your way to this point, you already know more than most about wine history, wine styles, winemaking, and wine in general.

So now you might consider getting serious. Not crazy, not over the top or beyond the pale, or however one might put it, but, hmm ... deliberate. Moving on to the next level. Donning the cloak of impassioned fan, if you will, a perfectly acceptable status minus the connotations of extremism as would be encountered in a wine snob, wine snot, or the often overbearing wine geek. The purpose in moving up the ladder is never to look down on those below. It is, instead, to enrich your own life, to examine, explore, and build your knowledge and your comfort level. The point, kids, is to sharpen your palate, to exercise your taste and smell apparatuses. To analyze, assess, and thereby enhance your wine drinking experience.

It only makes sense: the more you perceive and understand what you're swallowing, the more appreciative you will be when it's good and the more easily you will recognize when it's not. Life is short—why wallow in mediocrity when a bit of training and effort can help you separate the excellent from the average, the oh-so-fine from the merely so-so?

We discussed in Chapter Twelve the value of taking notes, of paying attention to what's in your glass, of assessing its olfactory and gustatory characteristics. Of course, you have done all this with the bottle in front of you, determining how much, and why, you do or don't enjoy a particular wine. Is it worthy of another purchase? Should you consider multiple bottles, maybe pick up a case? Or was this wine not really to your liking? Okay as part of a tasting lineup but hardly in the running for a return engagement?

If you've joined a tasting group or started one of your own or blind-tasted a lineup of Pinot Noirs to see which goes best with grilled salmon (or read Chapter Six!), there's a good chance you're already familiar with the bottle-in-a-bag technique. But this time, instead of just selecting your favorite wine from a known group, or assessing similarities and differences in a lineup of Merlots from various regions around the world, why not put yourself to the test and, if you're like me, have a good chuckle at the same time?

The final achievement in the universe of wine tasting (think "weekend warrior climbs Mt. Everest," though without the huffing and puffing or danger of being swept away by an icy avalanche, and you'll get some idea of the average success ratio) is to blind-taste complete mystery wines and try to identify them as to vintage, varietal, and region. This is the peak, where all your vinous knowledge and experience come together, where your understanding of color, aroma, taste, texture, and their myriad connections to age, grape variety, vintage temperatures, acid levels, even regional or stylistic idiosyncrasies narrows the field of possibilities and leads you to a clear and unequivocal conclusion regarding the contents of your glass.

Hmmm ... or not.

There are few things in the world more difficult to achieve than correctly identifying a completely unknown wine. When you don't know price, region, vintage, source, or anything else about a wine, guessing what's in the glass in front of you is a humbling experience. And it's this that gives rise to the humor. What else can you do but laugh when you "pinpoint" a wine as New World, probably Grenache from California's Central Coast, vintage 2013, and it is revealed to be a 2010 Super Tuscan from Italy, composed of 85% Sangiovese and 15% Merlot? Talk about deflating a swollen ego.

Such embarrassing moments, however, are an integral part of life in the advanced wine lane. A good point can be made that blind tasting of this sort accomplishes nothing, that's it's just a lame competition or the wine world's equivalent of a parlor game. For the casual drinker, that may be true, and yet there is much to be learned by subjecting yourself to this kind of sensory abuse. It causes you to hone your palate, to improve your sensitivity to acid, alcohol, sugar, and tannins, and to primary (from the fruit), secondary (from the fermentation), and tertiary (from the aging and maturation) flavors and aromas.

These are the skills used daily by winemakers and vignerons around the world to assess and analyze, to direct their next steps, to let them know what has been done right and what may need adjustment in the wines they are creating. For the importer, these skills can point to wines that should travel well and have further aging potential. The restaurateur wants to select wines that pair well with foods, especially the foods his or her kitchen turns out. Sommeliers want to understand the components of the wines they deal with so as to better recommend a wine based on a diner's taste profile as well as menu choice. Writers need the ability to discuss a wine more intelligently than to say merely that it's tasty or it's not.

Every facet of a wine tells something of the wine's back story, of its grape variety, of its provenance, the climate and conditions of its terroir, of its winemaker's approach, its fermentation, aging, and additives, of its storage conditions, in what vessel and for how long. Color, clarity, viscosity, aroma, sweetness, weight, taste and texture, tannins, acid, alcohol, and finish.

If you can taste with focus, without distraction, and know what to look for, the wine will speak. You may not always pick the right grape variety, but you will be able to eliminate many of them and narrow the possibilities. You may not nail the vintage, but you'll likely be within a year or two. The exact region may or may not be obvious, but if you miss it you'll choose another with very similar characteristics. With some practice you will start to get one or even two of the triumvirate correct, and now and again you will get them all. Extremely good tasters can determine the grape, the year, and not just the right country or region but even the right appellation, sometimes down to the specific producer!

Of course, such facility is rare, and no matter who you are, expect to get more wrong than not. But you will have a great time, you will challenge yourself, you'll have more than a few laughs, and you will learn so much more than tasting from a bottle that's known to you can ever convey.

Though I don't normally make recommendations, I have found three books to be of immense value in this arena. Most well-known, accomplished wine writers have at least one book on the market about wine tasting, and many of them are quite good. This small selection is less well-known and will be perhaps a bit more difficult to find, but if you'd really like to train your taster, to get hard-core, so to speak, the techniques and explanations presented in these volumes are invaluable.

The first is *How to Taste Wine*, by Pierre Casamayor, published in the United Kingdom by Cassell Illustrated. The second is *Making Sense of Wine Tasting*, by Alan Young, originally published by the Wine Appreciation Guild and now available through Board and Bench Publishing in the United States. And the third tasting tome extraordinaire is *Tasting & Grading Wine*, by Clive S. Michelsen, a publication of JAC International AB of Sweden that is also handled in the United States by Board and Bench Publishing.

So get into that serious tasting group, look for some advanced classes, or pick up one or all of these outstanding books and rev up your oenological engines. Ladies and gentlemen, it's time to taste wine!

FORTY-FIVE
FORTY-FIVE

GO DEEP, AND NARROW
(EXPERTISE AWAITS)

A GREAT SENSE OF ACCOMPLISHMENT COMES WITH HAVING or developing true expertise. Learning can, if allowed, offer a base of knowledge that's broad and shallow, knowing a little about a lot, having a superficial understanding of many subjects of interest without becoming expert in any of them. An educational jack-of-all, master-of-none, if you will. Such a generalist approach concerning "all things wine" may be sufficient in the company of friends lacking a genuine curiosity about wine or grapes or other such topics, perhaps coming into play only when confronted by a wine list at the restaurant where you're all dining together. "Here, you know wine. Pick out something good." And voilà, they leave it you to select the alcohol of the evening. After all, you do know more than they, and they'd rather not have the responsibility. A pleasing choice is rewarded with "Hey, this is good. You really know your stuff," while a selection less to their liking elicits a response along the lines of "Yeah, not bad. I guess. But you know I'm not much of a wine drinker."

Hardly a ringing endorsement of your enthusiasm or passion for the subject. Consider, the more you learn about and enjoy wine, the more time you'll spend with others who do as well, so why not go deep and focus on some particularly appealing aspect of wine instead of the once-over mile-wide and inch-deep approach? If there's one thing that aficionados love—besides a bottle of something lauded and applauded that they have never tried—it's a tidbit of information, a fact or figure or fragment, a story or background or explanation of some wine-related topic that is new to them. Tapping into a deeper level of learning by listening to what you're sharing. Now that's fun. And that's what they embrace with sometimes surprising gusto.

No matter how new or unused to the wine-appreciation scene you may be, bring something interesting, esoteric, or previously unknown to the table and you'll be welcomed by those already seated and waiting to pour. Acolytes of the holy juice are inclusive; they *want* fellow partisans to join them, to drink and enjoy and discuss wine with. Hence, expand your own expertise, latch on to some facet of wine lore that intrigues or compels you, and you can practically guarantee yourself an invite to the inner circle.

You may have an interest in family sagas, in business or commerce, in plants, gardening, or horticulture, in organic chemistry, in engineering or equipment design. You may be a history buff; a chef, a bartender, or a foodie; a drone enthusiast (think aerial sensors and vineyard mapping); a student of human physiology; a party host or hostess (with the mostess), a teacher, a geologist or geographer. Your field may be religion or international trade or foreign languages. Regardless, wine awaits you. And whatever your interest, wine provides a richness of knowledge and experience that few other subjects afford. In wine there is continuity, connectedness, a continuum of

human history and interaction that is part delight, part amazement, and part abject appreciation.

The more you know about wine, the more encompassing it becomes. Pick your focus, polish your facet. From the most concrete—science, trellising, fermentation, economics—to the most esoteric—religion, social lubricant, love, poetry—wine offers itself to your particular interest and allows you in-depth exploration. It's a rich and meaty subject, many-layered in many ways.

So become the expert. Develop unparalleled insight in the area that intrigues you most. Read and explore. Question and visit and put yourself in front of the train. The "wow" moments will come one after another. The joy of learning will fill you, and the perhaps-even-greater joy of sharing will cause your cup to gurgle over. We're beyond beginner here. And joyfully so.

A sampling of "specialty" wine books: the study of a dynasty, the science of oenology, the latest discoveries about ancient wines. From left to right, *The House of Mondavi*, by Julia Flynn Siler, *The Science of Wine*, by Jamie Goode, and *Ancient Wine*, by Patrick McGovern.

Wine is for everyone. Become one of those people the rest of us can turn to for insight and information. If you know about soils and their chemistry and composition and influence on vine growth and wine quality, if you can educate us in this area alone, we will appreciate you and never expect you to shine a light on the ancient history of wine as well.

Tell us about rivers and oceans and transport and trade routes and how wine was and is dispersed and distributed and which countries opened their markets to wines from elsewhere and how and why that changed their cultures and we will sit in rapt attention to your words and never fault you for your dearth of learnedness concerning fermentations in wood versus concrete versus steel, or the influence of French oak versus American versus Slovonian, or any other thing aside from your area of expertise.

The reality is that true wine geeks are cognizant of wine's expansive footprint and realize that no one, no matter how long or hard they study, can ever master its many components. So we develop a heartfelt appreciation for specific, drilled-down detail that sheds new light on the subject closest to our hearts. A nugget here, an insight about this or that, the kind of thing only someone who has studied wine can provide. We take our knowledge vicariously simply because there is too much to absorb it all directly.

Enjoy what excites you. Study and learn ever more about whatever aspects of wine most capture your attention and curiosity. And be sure to share, for therein lies your value to the community, to the great wide world of wine lovers. Thanks for your time and your energy and your interest. And pull up a chair—welcome to the group. Cheers to us all!

46

FORTY-SIX

FORTY-SIX

GET YOUR TOURIST GROOVE ON

IN SOME QUARTERS THE DESIGNATION "TOURIST" GETS A BAD rap. One shouldn't forget that the term is derived from *tour*— i.e., *an extended journey, usually taken for pleasure, visiting points of interest or significance along the way*. Which sounds to me rather like an admirable, educational, even enjoyable use of time. How else are we to know the world, to comprehend its splendors, its sights and sounds, its smells and textures and energy without actually being there, our senses open and alert and processing? How else to absorb the buzz of the crowds in the street, the smells of city or sea, the beauty of the landscape, the drama of historical monuments or ancient ruins?

There is no requirement of shorts worn with socks and sandals, or T-shirts emblazoned with pictures of fuzzy animals or local landmarks. A tourist blends in, or fails to, depending on his or her own sensibilities. There is no need for sunburned faces, fanny packs, or

It doesn't matter how fancy the accommodations.

selfie sticks; these silly quirks hardly define a tourist. The true *tourist* learns and absorbs, visits, assesses, and adds to his or her growing bank of knowledge and worldly experience.

What's more, if we're to speak of wine tourism in particular, as we probably should, a wonderful balance of nature and industry, of leisure and attention unfolds before us. There's more here than simply visiting a winery. There are new sights and surroundings, new cities and towns, new people and cultures, new food and drink, new sunsets and sunrises. Head to San Francisco, drive north along the coast, check into your room at Bodega Bay, enjoy dinner and wine as the sun sets over the harbor, let the sounds of the sea wake you and guide you to the mouth of the Russian River, and then follow its winding path upstream through lovely wooded hills to winery after winery. Or fly to Florence, let yourself be whisked away to an ancient villa where you relax by the pool, listen to the birds, and await a fabulous dinner. Awake to caffè Italiano, and then head off to sample some fabulous Chiantis and spend the day with local winemakers. Perhaps the next day you behold the Duomo, the Uffizi, stroll the medieval streets, stop by the Galleria dell'Accademia and gaze at Michelangelo's *David*. And then there's day three and day four, followed by five, and Chianti will never again taste or mean the same to you.

It's obvious that we could go on and on discussing the possible venues and variations of agritourism, enotourism, vinitourism, whatever you choose to call it. You might stay at an inexpensive hotel, motel, or Airbnb in a wine region you'd like to know better; you might find a room at the inn of a winery itself, meals and tours of surrounding wineries included; or, for those with a Champagne budget, why not splurge on the oh-so-fine wine country resort and spa and all the attendant amenities, and wine, that money can buy? The point is that whether your choice is low-rent or high-roller, you can enjoy a fabulous time getting to know the food and wine, the culture and countryside of just about any wine region in the world.

Traveling to these wine lands tends to funnel one through the world's great cities and into landscapes of jaw-dropping beauty. San Francisco leads to Napa Valley and the Sonoma Coast. Rome takes

Ah, Tuscany ...

us to Florence, to the vineyards of Tuscany, Umbria, and Abruzzo. From Paris one visits Champagne and Bordeaux and the left and right banks. Madrid guides us to Rioja; Barcelona to Priorat. From Buenos Aires we visit Mendoza and the Uco Valley. Cape Town leads to Stellenbosch, Franschhoek, and Paarl. Vancouver welcomes us to the Okanagan; Lyon to the Rhone. Christchurch is our gateway to the Waipara Valley and Central Otago. And it's not just wine; it's cuisine and culture and history and geography. It's an education, with drinks.

And lest we overlook the natural and man-made wonders lurking nearby, consider the plethora of non-vinous sites our wine travels likewise afford us. Depending on route and mode of travel, if you're heading to Napa or other northern California wine regions, the Golden Gate Bridge, Fisherman's Wharf, Chinatown, and Point Reyes are all right there to greet you. Canada's Ontario wine country puts you on the shores of Lake Ontario, just minutes from Niagara

Vines of Mendoza, Uco Valley, Argentina

Falls, an hour from Toronto. The bustle of Milan and the beauty of the Italian Alps line the way to Piemonte, while Rome itself, one of humankind's most significant creations, welcomes visitors bound for most of Italy's wine regions. An extra day, or a month if you can, turns your wine tour into an adventure of unforgettable richness.

Thinking of Mendoza or other Argentine regions? Say hello to Buenos Aires, to the Casa Rosada, to the pampas, to the best steaks in the world, to Iguazu Falls. Or if Chile is on the radar, be prepared for the magnificent Andes, Santiago, and the UNESCO World Heritage Site of Valparaiso.

Spain's regions welcome you to every corner of that vibrant country, from Andalusia and its gifts of flamenco, the Alcázar of Seville and the magical Alhambra; to Barcelona and its Sagrada Familia, Museu Picasso, and Fundació Joan Miró; to Bilbao and San Sebastian, offering what many consider the most exquisite restaurants in the world and Gehry's stunning Guggenheim Museum; and finally to Galicia, home of Spain's rugged verdant coast and terminus of the Camino de Santiago.

Set aside as many days as you can. Be a tourist, reinvigorate and revive. At the very least such a trip is R&R for the body, but so often it renews the spirit and restores the soul, as well.

We've not spoken of Austria, of its breathtaking peaks and the glories of Vienna; nor of Paris, of the Louvre, La Tour Eiffel, the cobbled streets, the neighborhoods and bistros. Greece, oh my—islands, beaches, history, monuments, ruins, and museums. Germany, Australia, Croatia. And India: new to the world of wine but offering everything else a traveler could hope for. So many countries, so much to see, to absorb, to immerse oneself in, so close to so many vineyards and wineries. Portugal, Hungary, Georgia. Switzerland, Peru, Mexico, and Brazil. Always focused on the wines, the grapes and styles and winemakers who ensure that Bacchus' gifts continue to give, but never ignoring the companion sites, and sights, that curious, hungry eyes and minds devour like sustenance.

Do, however, call or e-mail ahead of time—a week or two should suffice—to the wineries at the top of your list. Not all wineries are open to visitors at all times; some are never open to the public, especially outside the United States, without an appointment. But a quick e-mail—"We are fans of your wine and would very much like to visit the winery on such-and-such a date"—will more often than not put you on the fast track to welcomed-guest status. Don't be surprised if the owner or winemaker greets you personally and arranges a special tasting. These busy people will greatly appreciate your thoughtfulness.

And as a courtesy to yourself, I highly recommend hiring a driver. Take it from someone who used to drive everywhere, through the back roads of Spain, up and down

the hills of Piemonte, from Walla Walla to Paso Robles, in search of the next winery on my list, that being able to sit back and "rest" your eyes between stops, to marvel at the scenery and not worry about the route or whether you've had a touch too much to taste, is a wonderful luxury. It's safer, it's smarter, and wine country drivers often know more about the wineries and the surroundings than your guidebook is ever going to tell you. Go online or ask the front desk

On the way to South Africa's Cape winelands

or concierge at your hotel for names and recommendations. You'll be glad you did, and if you're like me, you'll wonder why you hadn't chosen this route sooner.

Another option is to locate a local wine tour, especially if you're just passing through an area or haven't had a chance to do much research. Tours may be just you and your partner driven to a set lineup of local wineries, usually with a stop for lunch somewhere on the schedule, or as many as five or six fellow wine fanciers sharing a van and the pleasure of each other's company. These can be great fun; you will often find yourself sipping and swapping stories with folks from around the world, entertaining each other while the driver takes care of business.

But however you do it, do it. Trips to wine country, vacations in the vineyards of wine regions near and far, are among the oenophile's greatest pleasures. Wine covers much of human history and thrives in most of the great civilizations of past and present. So bite off your own chunk of the wine-dark world and savor every swallow. You're gonna love it!

FORTY-SEVEN
FORTY-SEVEN

REMEMBER AND ASSOCIATE

A S WE ALL KNOW, OUR SMELLER, WHICH IN LARGE PART IS also our taster, is directly wired into our rememberer, i.e., those portions of the brain more formally referenced as the amygdala and hippocampus, most responsible for memory and emotion. Kind of an odd arrangement, if you think about it. But the hard truth is that smells, aromas, are first run through the gauntlet of memory and emotion before reaching other portions of the brain. The connection between smell and memory and emotion is primal and undeniable. Before ever assessing a smell (or taste, since what we call "flavor" is primarily the impact of volatile substances on the olfactory epithelium, which comprises much of the upper nasal cavity) for objective characteristics like fruit, floral, savory, sweet, or mineral elements, our brains respond to any history we may have tucked away with similar-smelling substances and the accompanying emotions or reactions they originally generated.

Hence, if you got terribly drunk on tequila one night long ago in your wayward youth, the simple act of smelling tequila may cause you to feel ill, repelled by an odor that carries a strong negative association. You would be hard put to complete an objective tasting of tequila, to assess strengths and weaknesses and comparisons of one tequila to another.

Perhaps you've noticed how some folks despise the smell of tobacco while others are drawn to it. It's an odor that elicits strong reactions, dependent almost entirely on one's personal exposure to it at some point in the past.

That's why memory and associations are so important to tasting. A Pinot Noir that's redolent of red fruit and spices may pinball

The scent of tobacco may trigger fond memories of Grandpa.

through your sniffer and evoke flashbacks of your grandmother's incredibly delicious cherry pie, a very positive emotional connection. Fair to say that you are going to like that particular Pinot. On the other hand, the licorice of a Priorat may tickle an emotional

Who can forget the aroma of Grandma's cherry pie?

memory of your mean old aunt giving neighbor kids sticks of licorice but denying them to you because you hadn't behaved properly. That slight was buried deep in your memory and its resurrection brings back feelings of exclusion and denial. Though you may ultimately credit the Priorat with being well-made or well-balanced, there is a good chance it will never be among your favorites.

Knowing this, we're more able to deal with the phenomenon, known as "odor-evoked autobiographical memory," and use it to our advantage. It is, in fact, a way to pin down a wine for future reference.

Whenever I taste a good Merlot or a good Rioja, it puts me in mind of chocolate-covered cherries, a special treat of childhood. Someone else may argue with my assessment, but their perception has no relevance; it's my brain using my experience to analyze what I'm tasting. And it provides an inside edge in blind tastings.

But the best use of this interesting trick of the brain may be to court it proactively. When next your nose is sunk into the airspace of a glass containing wine and you wish to either recall that specific pour, or the surroundings where you are located (the vineyard, winery, or other picturesque locale), or the people in whose company you are drinking, inhale a healthy whiff of wine scent and consciously imprint and associate the juice, the place, and the people with the smells your brain is ingesting.

It won't work as effortlessly as the scents of childhood were able to imprint themselves on your gray matter and henceforth recall specific memories and emotions, but if you truly focus and think it as you do it, there will be some effect. Odors are a great assist in reminding us of the past, much more so than cues from sights or sounds alone.

You can even boost your "scent consciousness" by, yes, taking time to smell the roses—in a manner of speaking. Actually, make a point of smelling everything: your food before you eat it, the scent of flowers or cut grass, summer rains or fallen leaves. Smell the odors of your job. These might include ink and paper or grease and diesel or leather and wood. Smell fruit and spices and coffee and all manner of things as you come across them during your day, and night. If we worked at developing our sense of smell a tenth as much as we develop and maintain and refer to the world around us by means of sight, we would be formidable.

How cool to instantly harken back to a lazy picnic with your sweetheart in Provence whenever you nose a rosé of Mourvèdre, or to remember your wedding reception with every glass of Perrier-Jouet Grand Brut and its creamy apple and vanilla notes. Personally, I cannot sip or savor a glass of Juan Gil Monastrell without recalling a particular dinner in a particular little restaurant in Bilbao many years ago.

Truthfully, if you served this same wine to me blind, I might fail to make the association, or if you poured me a completely different Spanish Monastrell I might yet swear I was back at dinner in Basque Country. Monastrells do and can resemble one another. Working to enhance memories and associations is intended neither as a clever trick nor a scientific certainty. It's simply another weft of fabric in the tapestry of our wine lives.

It encourages us to pay a bit more attention to what we're drinking when we're drinking it, and to fit wine and our wine experiences into the greater context of life. When something is very good, it just makes sense to lower the barriers and let it flow more deeply into the essence of who we are and what we have experienced and enjoyed. Or, if I may paraphrase—love me now, love me forever.

FORTY-EIGHT
FORTY EIGHT

NO, REALLY … FIND FAULT

Yes, this is a book about the inherent goodness, the pleasure and joy, of all things wine. So why focus on finding fault or pointing out those wines that do not please us, wines that we might think too sweet or too dry, or too boring or too pricey?

Actually, sweet and dry, common or costly are personal preferences and external perceptions—important, yes, but neither fault nor flaw in the wine itself. Rather they are characteristics of style, on the one hand, and marketing or economics, on the other. If we think a wine is overly sweet or too expensive, it's easy enough to simply refrain from purchasing it.

The faults we do need to address, however, are those caused by missteps in the making or handling of wine that degrade or destroy the product. Whether you buy chocolate milk or regular is a choice, but if the milk you bring home is sour, you have encountered a product ruined by faulty production, storage, or temperature control somewhere along the way from pasture to store shelf. These are the kinds of faults that one should understand and be able to identify. Some may be worse than others but all are mistakes or oversights that result in damaged goods. As consumers, we shouldn't be expected to foot the bill for subpar products. No one would accept delivery of a new car with a flat tire or a dozen eggs with cracked shells.

You will notice, for instance, if you watch a sommelier at work or a group of professional tasters, be they wine judges, winemakers, or wine buyers at a trade tasting, that their first look and sniff is simply to establish the soundness of the wine, even before they dive into a full evaluation. If a wine they're assessing is bubbly and shouldn't be, or turgid when it should be clear, if it smells of sulfur or wet dog, the red flags go up. These are signs of problems, of faults that may or may not make the wine undrinkable but that certainly reduce its quality and appeal.

Whether you are buying wine by the glass at a local bar or restaurant or by the bottle, either online or from a retailer, you have the right to get what you pay for—a clean, sound, unflawed representation of what's on the label. And like everything else with wine, you have to first pay attention and develop your sensory awareness until identifying the presence of such faults becomes second nature.

But worry not; we have no interest in getting into the very complicated chemistry of what causes specific wine faults, who or what is responsible, and how they can be avoided. If we can just tell that a wine *is* faulty, we can send it back and get a replacement. And no restaurant or wine shop of any value will give you a hard time about this. If a wine is bad—and everyone comes across a bad wine from time to time—they return it to the distributor. Or, if it's their fault, then it's their fault, but they still have an obligation to sell untainted product.

The first place to be on the lookout is at the bar or dining room where you have just ordered a glass of something to ease you into

A Coravin lets you pour a glass of anything
without compromise.

the evening. If possible, take a big whiff from the bowl of the wine glass before anything is poured into it. You may be surprised to get a bleach or dish detergent smell. It's not unusual for a commercial dishwasher to have a weak rinse cycle or to be loaded with too much soap. Nothing ruins wine more quickly that a poorly cleaned or rinsed glass. If you don't have a chance to smell the glass before the wine is poured, at least take a hefty sniff before you drink it. A strong aroma of bleach wafting up through the wine says, "Send me back!"

The next common fault of wine-by-the-glass programs is that of oxidation. Is your glass of Château Wishitwasbetter showing a bit of brown or orange around the rim, or smelling and tasting cooked or tired with a sort of nutty, Sherry-like scent to it? Is it flat and without interest? Has it lost the fruit and vibrancy normally associated with that particular cuvee? If so, it has probably been open for too long (even stored properly, most bottles survive only a day, maybe two) and the invading oxygen has beaten your wine into a tired pool of worn-out juice, much like an apple slice that's been left out too long and turned an unlovely brown.

In fairness, it's difficult to maintain the freshness in a bottle of wine being sold by the glass. Ask your server when the bottle was uncorked and request the same wine poured from a newly opened bottle. The difference will be amazing. Quite honestly, a good-quality by-the-glass program can use inert gas or even a nifty little device known as a Coravin to serve you consistently fresh and intact wine. Either approach is a small investment to ensure a sound product for their customers.

It's true these first two "faults" were more the result of sloppiness in washing and leaving an open bottle around for too long, but these are common occurrences you are likely, sooner or later, to encounter at many bars and restaurants.

Another fault you may come across is the odor of vinegar or acetone. In small amounts, especially in red wine, this is fairly harmless and points to an eventual defect rather than indicating a currently undrinkable wine. VA, as it's called, or volatile acidity, indicates a wine early in its transition from juice to vinegar. Some drinkers don't mind it, some don't even notice it, and others will find it completely off-putting.

On the other hand, the presence of excess sulfur compounds is something no one likes. All wine contains a bit of sulfur, as the fermentation process itself generates small amounts of it, but if that wonderful, big sniff used to greet a glass of wine jerks your head back with the tingling pungency of burnt matches or rotten eggs (mmm, sounds delish, no?) instead of the lovely fruit aromas you were expecting, it's a good bet you've got a dumper, as in down the drain. Swirl it around and give it a few minutes to blow off, which it sometimes will. But if it hangs around beyond that, I'd head for the sink.

Unless … you've just poured a German Riesling, often bottled with a larger-than-necessary dose of sulfur as protection against spoilage. Additionally, Mosel Rieslings, due to yeasts, fermentation methods, etc., are known to occasionally suffer from a condition called "reduction," an absence of oxygen that likewise creates rotten egg aromas. It's claimed that the bottling sulfur will eventually break down and disappear, if you live that long. As to the smell of reduction, you might try being a good Riesling drinker: hold your nose, figuratively only, of course, and drink. Under that funk often lies some mighty fine wine.

Are you enjoying this "faults" stuff? Kind of fun, isn't it? And though you would think otherwise, it does make a person love wine more. I think it's the inside look, the vulnerability, the individuality or quirkiness it exposes that makes wine that much dearer to the heart. Anyway ...

On to Brettanomyces, known to friend and foe alike as Brett, an outlaw yeast, a drifter who moseys into perfectly happy little wineries and starts pushing the other yeast around. A rogue, if you will. Known to seduce winemakers with aromas of leather and bacon fat and maybe a little spicy clove. All good. Adds to the complexity and character of the resulting wine. Until it gets out of hand.

Then our "friend" tries to take over, and the real Brett shows himself. Smells like a barnyard—you wonder what's on his boots— and those cheap band-aids always getting flicked into the fermenter. Yuck. No respect. Pretty soon the whole shooting match smells like a dog park. If you got a bottle while he was still in his smiley "Yes, ma'am," "Oh, absolutely, sir" phase, you probably have a doggone tasty bottle of wine there. But if you were a little slow to the party, chances are good the wine is bad. As in "Whew. Kinda stinky, kinda nasty. Think I'll send this one back."

Then there are times when you stick your nose into a glass of wine and get the exquisite aromas of moldy basement, wet cardboard, or old mushrooms. Fortunately, cork taint, aka TCA, aka 2,4,6-trichloroanisole, which stems from an undetectable fungus in the cork, is less common than it once was (see Chapter Thirty-Seven for more). But when it's there in concentrations high enough for you to notice, it signifies a bottle irretrievably compromised. The wine will be flat and lifeless and may taste like cardboard instead of the plums and cherries you had been expecting. The only alternative is to return the faulty bottle. With the industry's improved understanding of how to clean, and not clean, corks and wineries both, TCA these days seldom infects more than a random, occasional bottle.

Wine is an amazingly complex, fragile, and ever-changing substance. There's far more chemistry occurring in a tank or bottle of wine than even the chemists understand. Anything foreign that's introduced into or that affects the wine initiates a chain of events or reactions that alter its makeup. Fungi, bacteria, oxygen, yeasts, oak lignin, and lactones all find their way into wines, some welcome, some not. It is part of the winemaker's job to control this inflow, to let in the good and keep out the bad, and in the right proportions.

Once it leaves the winery, this critical stewardship is passed on to a variety of exporters, importers, distributors, retailers, et al. Some acknowledge their responsibility to the product, while others consider wine merely another SKU to move along the supply chain. And that kind of thinking can be damaging, especially as regards controlling temperature.

Wine likes a cool environment, one that keeps unwanted chemical reactions to a minimum. It's not big on sunshine, either, or being stored next to the stove or up in the attic. Yet some folks, too concerned with pinching pennies to engage a reefer, are willing to transport wine in the back of a broiling unrefrigerated truck or an uninsulated metal container on the deck of a ship. Just as bad is the retailer who has a display of wine next to the glass storefront where it can cook and soak up the afternoon sun.

Cooked wine is entirely avoidable, which in one sense makes it more egregious than sulfur problems or cork taint. A couple of dollars and some common sense would eliminate the problem completely. Beware of young white wines that look distressingly brown, reds that have a cheap jammy aroma, or any wine that tastes nutty with Sherry- or Madeira-like notes to it. A cooked wine smells, well, cooked. And tastes lousy. Flat, strangely like caramel, maybe with a little volatile acidity starting to rear its ugly head.

Whatever the problem, it should first be realized that everything has imperfections. More so, perhaps, for agricultural products that go through many steps and stages to reach their final iteration. And with wine, even that continues to morph and evolve. The true miracle is that we have so much very good, unflawed wine from which to choose, whether it be for tonight's dinner or to lay down for future enjoyment. There was a time when "faulty" wine, by modern standards, was commonplace. But no longer. Wine has never been better. In fact, it's fair to say that we live in the golden age of wine, worldwide, in terms of both quantity and quality.

Gotta love that.

49

FORTY-NINE

FORTY-NINE

FIND A WAY TO PASS IT ON

E NEAR THE END. IF YOU HAVE EMBRACED, EXPLORED, or fiddled with any or all of the many ways to love wine outlined herein, you possess a thing of more than passing value. This knowledge, this experience, is a chunk of the good stuff that many still, sadly, live without. You've tasted Finos and Fianos, visited wineries, maybe sabered a bottle or two of Champagne, discovered some lesser- to previously unknown grape varieties. Whatever you were motivated to pursue—a tasting group? Retsina? older vintages?—has added drops, if not buckets, to your font of oenological wisdom. And so we learn, by dribs and drabs, a slow-rolling accumulation much like that of an old dented tractor sweeping up golf balls at a second-rate driving range. The difference being, however, that instead of collecting homogenous spheres of little to no consequence, we are in fact gathering nuggets of pleasure, explosions of information, tidbits of delight, if not soupcons of awareness and sensibility. To wit, like it or not, you have become a keeper of the key.

And as such, it is now your duty, though it should be looked on more as a privilege, to pass on whatever morsels of vinous happiness you have acquired to others less fortunate, grape-wise, than yourself.

Key? you ask. *What key? And pass what? To whom?*

Ah, good questions, all. The key to your personal storehouse of knowledge, just down the path from where one enters and walks the long, rambling, and very pleasing, in fact, at times exciting, continuum of human/wine synchronicity. And to whom? Well, to your friends, of course. To your neighbors and acquaintances, your family and co-workers. To any and all within that circle of interpersonal ripples that we generate by tossing ourselves into the pond of life.

It can be quite low-key. When next you have some friends—BFFs, cohorts, running buddies, chicas, homies, goombahs—stop by for a visit, for a glass and a chat, give them something orange rather than red or white, and share with them the story of what they are drinking and how it came to be. Having Sunday dinner with the folks? Maybe a sibling or two, or siblings and spouses involved? Why not tote along a magnum or even a Jeroboam if enough thirsty palates are expected? Spread the smiles, let the questions blossom.

Post some pics of you and the current better half sipping something wonderful at the winery, any winery, and throw in a few words about the juice, the people, and the place. Make someone else wanna be there. Tell them what they're missing. Engender curiosity.

Let them know—all of them, your friends and family and whoever enters your orbit—that you're learning and you're loving it. Wine is so enhanced by company and sharing; keep a few good to extremely intriguing bottles around, at the ready, for any fertile conglomerations of taste buds that might happen through your door, whatever their reason for being there. Surprise them—sit them down and proffer a pour. Become known for your hospitality and enthusiasm. It will, as you know, all come back to thank you.

Or ... it needn't be low-key at all. An expanding knowledge of and exposure to fine wine has been known to stimulate major life changes. Stories abound of waitresses and prep cooks bitten by the bug who change course and go on to become highly regarded sommeliers, of scientists who give up their careers to return to school and study winemaking, of seasoned journalists who decide that writing about wine beats reporting the nightly news. Wine is not to be feared but embraced.

Post some pics—let them know you're loving it.

While you may not be on the verge of saying adieu to the job that's paying your rent or mortgage, you can still pass on your rather substantial wine knowledge (assuming, clearly, that you've read all the chapters! wink, wink) in a profusion of meaningful ways. You might, for instance, teach a class at a local adult education program. Wine is a perennially popular topic, and many of these informal institutions are in constant need of good instructors. And teaching, it should be said, is a great way to energize your own learning. Put together a few sample classes. Start with something simple like reds vs. whites, or New World vs. Old, and you'll see what I mean.

If teaching isn't your thing, start a tasting group. Designate a theme for each get-together and structure your tastings so there's time for discussion about the wines being sampled. Offer to do a tasting for your company or residents of the building you live in. Find a blog (or start your own) or a local newspaper that is willing to use an article about wine that you write, maybe turn it into a regular thing.

Get a part-time job pouring wine samples at liquor stores, wine shops, or grocery stores. Many of these positions are only a few hours a week and can easily fit in with your full-time gig. They are a great way to both pass on wine info to customers and be exposed to wines you might not otherwise encounter. If you enjoy this kind of interaction with consumers, you might also consider working at a wine bar or picking up a regular shift in a wine store or wine department somewhere.

The options are many. It's fun to discuss wine, to sip and savor with friends and acquaintances, to see the delight in the eyes of the initiated when you pull out the corkscrew, wipe off the label of something they have never seen, and tell them you have been waiting for the right person to share this with.

There is always more to learn, more to know, more to absorb and understand about wine. Some folks become specialists, in a region, in viticulture, in viniculture, in service, in sales, in history, in tasting. Others just love the drinking, and the sharing. There is no right or wrong. Whether wine is your full-time vocation or your occasional chill pill after a hard day at the grist mill hardly matters. Because it is still, in either case, a gift from nature, from the gods of life and renewal, from Geshtinanna of Sumeria, Siduri of Babylon, Renenutet and Shesmu of Egypt, Teshub, the Hittite, Dionysus of Greece or Bacchus in his Roman incarnation. Wine is the product of renewal, of vines seemingly gone dead in the winter, laden with fruit mere months later. It is a mystery, and a blessing.

So pass on what you know, what you have learned, so that our lineage, begun so very long ago, will continue in its quest, in so many ways, to enrich ever more lives. You're no longer a rookie on the outside looking in; you're part of the program now. And who doesn't love that? Welcome to the circle.

BE A PHILOSOPHER

Put another way, do a few contemplative turns on the Rubik's cube of life. See how, if at all, the story lines of wine and human existence line up. No prelude here to professorship, merely a short, if sustained, flexing of the mental muscles in service of, how shall we say ... applying the mortar to those fifty lately laid, roughly hewn blocks so as to secure their position, not as a wall but rather a foundation on which to build, a stage on which to dance, a rostrum from which to declaim the glories, the complexities, the inherent happiness bequeathed of grape juice duly fermented and respectfully ingested.

Think about it, is all that's being said.

Spending a handful of moments pondering the ins and outs of truth, knowledge, and the meaning of life is, admittedly, no mean feat. So perhaps narrowing our focus would help. After all, one can apply the principles of philosophy to many snips and slices of life as we know and practice it. Google "The Philosophy of ... " and one instantly gets three hundred and some million hits, including such gems as the philosophy of Rick and Morty, the philosophy of *South Park*, the philosophy of the high jump, the philosophy of the kiss, and Bertrand Russell's ever-popular "The Philosophy of Logical Atomism." Leaving such mind-benders out of this particular lineup, one still encounters the more expected categories: i.e., the philosophies of ethics, education, history, society, science, sport, love, and, of course, the navel gazers' favorite, the philosophy of philosophy.

Clearly, if one can discourse on the philosophy of love, war, or consciousness, a similar examination of wine's influence on the human condition should be joyfully endorsed. Does wine not touch on all the main branches of philosophic inquiry? Recall that wine's earliest "formal" usage was to reveal an alternate reality, the dwelling place of the gods, that we—or those so enabled or encouraged to undertake the journey on our behalf—could receive guidance, instruction, and the assurance that powers greater than ourselves were directing the world around us. Ritual drunkenness took human minds to places seldom seen, beyond our normal ability to visit. Whether in the hut of a shaman or conjurer or within the mud-block temples of Sumer or Babylon, as priest or acolyte or privileged participant, one drank wine to excess not for entertainment but to encounter God. This was sacred duty.

Such direct study of the nature of reality and existence, of what is and isn't possible to know, are among the key concerns of philosophy. On a more prosaic level, the Greeks were greatly concerned not just with metaphysics or epistemology, but also with beauty and esthetics, ethics and pleasure: i.e., was beauty an objective or subjective quality? could the pursuit of pleasure be among our highest callings? Of course, these discussions, the very foundations of Western philosophy, took place, led famously by Pythagoras, Socrates, Plato, and other educated thinkers and citizens, during much-admired, designated drinking sessions known as *symposia.*

Kylix—standard two-handled drinking vessel of the Greeks

These after-dinner discussion groups are well-documented. Wine was served to begin the gathering and remained the focal point of activity, which typically also included intense debates on government and philosophy, the playing of music, recitations of poetry, and games of a sexual inclination. It was not unusual to discuss and determine how drunk the attendees should allow themselves to become on any given night. One doesn't usually consider the import of wine in the intellectual evolution of our culture, but without wine there would have been no symposia. Our society would have developed in quite a different way.

And then we have the "social lubricant" effect of wine. If being relaxed and enjoying your companions is a worthy goal, then surely wine is to be embraced. Or if honesty and truth-telling are high on your list of desirables, Pliny the Elder's words "in wine there is truth," must be given their due. Clearly, drinking wine removes social and cultural governors and inhibitions. How we behave when so relaxed and whether honesty should ever be subject to restraint are additional topics relevant to this philosophical discussion. But you needn't go that far. Some cogent thoughts about friendship, sharing, happiness, responsibility, and other such concerns, and how they relate to you and to wine, are perhaps less taxing though not likely to be less important. Behavior and interaction, the norms and our relationship to those norms, are probably going to be of more realistic and immediate concern to modern wine lovers than considerations of ritual drunkenness.

At the same time, we mustn't lose sight of accepting grapes and vineyards as part of creation, and wine as part of creation's bounty. Is it not intrinsic to the natural order that wine presents itself as a gift? Do those who stand in opposition to the consumption of wine deny the inherent benevolence of creation? Is wine not meant as an offering to gladden the human heart and to bring comfort and reassurance? These philosophical musings border on the religious—as they should—but are we to ignore the blessings and the community that wine has for so many eons provided to our species?

Applying standard philosophical methods to any question or concern is an excellent way to reset one's compass. Determine what is to be considered. The esthetics of wine? The influence of wine on happiness? How wine affects your relationship to food. To the object of your worship. To social interactions? To learning? To engagement with the world as a whole? Question your own beliefs and previous conclusions on the subject, if you have given them thought. Engage, either with yourself or others, in discussion on the topic, on the pros and cons, and finally, formulate a position, your position, one that satisfies who and what you are.

It can all be easier and more relaxed than it may sound. But wine inhabits a broad landscape. We've just looked at fifty ways to increase our enjoyment and appreciation of the sacred juice and, if anything, discovered what a huge topic it is. Surely, anything so deeply embedded in our psyche, our history, our sense of pleasure and joy, our relationship with the Almighty, is worth a few minutes of reflection. For that, and for sticking with me through this delightful journey, I love you all. Salud.

IMAGES AND ILLUSTRATIONS

CHAPTER 14

1 Basket vines, Santorini – ©VasilyMulyukin/Shutterstock
2 Worker pruning vines – courtesy of the author
3 Measuring Brix – courtesy Gisborne Peak Wines
4 Farm workers – courtesy Carolyn Corley Burgess

CHAPTER 15

1 Pouring into a decanter – ©g-stockstudio/Shutterstock
2 Decanting over light – photo by Kate Laughren

CHAPTER 17

1 Vintage opened bottles – courtesy of the author

CHAPTER 18

1 Workers sorting grapes – courtesy Lodi Wine Commission
2 Punching down the cap – courtesy Creation Wines
3 Cleaning bins – courtesy Tensley Wines

CHAPTER 20

1 Counterfeit Petrus – public domain/US Marshalls Service

CHAPTER 21

1 Hosing down winery – courtesy of the author
2 Cleaning out the fermenter – courtesy of the author
3 A master of Zinfandel – courtesy Klinkerbrick Winery
4 Industrial winery – ©Elena Luria/Dreamstime

CHAPTER 22

1 Sauternes – photo by Miguel Lecuona
2 Botrytis – courtesy Jamie Goode
3 Grapes drying on rack – courtesy Fiona Maclean

CHAPTER 23

1 Sherry velo cross section – courtesy Consejo Regulador Sherry y Manzanilla de Sanlúcar
2 Sherry solera – ©PhilipLange/Shutterstock
3 Sherry line-up – courtesy Consejo Regulador

CHAPTER 25

1 Riddling rack – photo by Gerald Weisl/weimax.com
2 Frozen yeast plug – courtesy gfwineblog.co.uk

CHAPTER 27

1 Languedoc vineyard – ©warpedgalerie/Fotolia.com
2 Mosel River – ©AM-C/iStock
3 Heat wave – ECMWF/CC BY-NC-ND 4.0

CHAPTER 28

1 Wine dinner – courtesy Rick Caruso

CHAPTER 29

1 Rosés – photo by Kate Laughren
2 Rosé store display – Seifert & Jones Wines/Teresa Schmidt

CHAPTER 30

1 King Ashurbanipal – Alamy Stock Photo

CHAPTER 33

1 Volunteers working – courtesy Total Wine & More
2 Harvest dinner – courtesy Dr. Liz Thach, MW/WineTravelStories.com

CHAPTER 34

1 Greek frieze – courtesy Dr. Richard Baxter
2 Antique kvevri – courtesy Wikimedia
3 Tinajas - ©Jerónimo Alba/Alamy Stock Photo
4 Foradori winery – courtesy Harald Hertz/FeelWineTeller.com
5 Glass of kvevri wine – ©spaswinefood

CHAPTER 36

1 Glass labware – ©LoveSilhouette/Shutterstock
2 Plastic labware – courtesy of the author
3 Wine blending set-up – courtesy wineexperience.org

CHAPTER 37

1 Amphorae – edella©123rf.com
2 Woman sniffing faulty wine – ©AdamGregor/ Dreamstime.com

CHAPTER 38

1 Orange wines – photo by Michelle Sun/Tasting Table
2 Cretan winemaking facility – OlafTausch/CC BY 3.0
3 Cap in kvevri – courtesy Giorgi Barisashvili

CHAPTER 40

1 Nosing the wine – ©Kareinoppe/Shutterstock
2 Wine seminar – courtesy Society of Wine Educators

CHAPTER 42

1 Friends enjoying wine – ©DarrenBaker/Shutterstock

CHAPTER 43

1 Wine and chocolate – photo by Kate Laughren;

CHAPTER 45

1 Wine books – courtesy of the author

CHAPTER 46

1 Inexpensive motel – R.Ben-Ari©123rf.com
2 Luxury hotel – ©M.Starychenko/Dreamstime.com

3 Tuscany – ©Lianem/Dreamstime
4 Mendoza resort – courtesy Vines of Mendoza/Vines Resort & Spa
5 Elephants – D.Steele©123rf.com

CHAPTER 47
1 Cigar in ashtray – courtesy HomeWetBar.com
2 Cherry pie – B.Hofacker©123rf.com

CHAPTER 48
1 Pouring from Coravin – photo by Max Flatow Photography

CHAPTER 49
1 Couple in chai – auremar©123rf.com

CHAPTER 50
1 Greek kylix – courtesy Harvard Art Museums

APPENDIX

GRAPE VARIETIES MENTIONED OR DISCUSSED

* numbered varieties are the same grape reflecting regional, national, or historical differences in naming

Agiorgitiko
Aglianico
Albariño
Alicante Bouschet
Aligoté
Arneis
Arbois
Assyrtiko
Baga
Barbera
Blaufränkisch
Bobal
Bonarda
Brachetto
Cabernet Franc
Cabernet Sauvignon
Cannonau[1]
Carménère
Carignan
Chambourcin
Chardonel
Chardonnay

Chasselas
Chenin Blanc
Cinsault
Cortese
Counoise
Dolcetto
Dornfelder
Erbaluce
Falanghina
Fiano
Frappato
Friulano
Furmint
Gaglioppo
Gamay
Garganega
Garnacha[1]
Gewürztraminer
Glera
Godello
Grechetto
Greco di Tufo

Grenache[1]
Grenache Blanc
Grignolino
Grillo
Grüner Veltliner
Hondarrabi Zuri
Kisi
Lagrein
Lambrusco
Listán Negro
Macabeo[2]
Magdeleine Noire des
Charentes
Malagousia
Malbec
Mandilaria
Marsanne
Melon de Bourgogne
Mencia
Merlot
Monastrell[3]
Montepulciano
Moscato
Moschofilero
Mourvèdre[3]
Mtsvane
Müller-Thurgau
Muscat
Muscatel
Nebbiolo
Negroamaro
Nerello Mascalese
Nero d'Avola
Norton

Palomino
Parellada
Pecorino
Pedro Jimenez
Pedro Ximénez
Petit Manseng
Petit Sirah
Petit Verdot
Picpoul
Pinotage
Pinot Bianco[4]
Pinot Blanc[4]
Pinot Grigio[5]
Pinot Gris[5]
Pinot Nero[6]
Pinot Noir[6]
Primitivo[7]
Pigato
Plavac Mali
Ribolla Gialla
Riesling
Rkatsiteli
Roditis
Sagrantino
Sangiovese
Saperavi
Sauvignon Blanc
Schiava
Sémillon
Shavkapito
Shiraz[8]
Spätburgunder[6]
Syrah[8]
Tannat

Tempranillo
Teroldego
Timorasso
Tinta Barroca
Torrontés
Touriga Nacional
Traminette
Trebbiano[9]
Ugni Blanc[9]
Verdejo
Verdicchio
Vermentino
Vidal Blanc
Viognier
Viura[2]
Xarel·lo
Xinomavro
Zinfandel[7]
Zweigelt

We hope you enjoyed "**50 Ways to Love Wine More.**"
If so, please take a minute to leave a review at Amazon.com
or the retail site where you purchased it.

Your contribution is greatly appreciated.

Also by Jim Laughren:

A Beer Drinker's Guide To Knowing And Enjoying Fine Wine

"tons of useful information ... fun to use and fun to read"
San Francisco Book Review

"an unintimidating yet rich tour through the world of wine"
Kirkus Review (starred)

Available from Amazon.com, Crosstownpublishing.com
and select bookstores

Visit www.jimlaughren.com for wine news and musings
and inside tips for wine, beer, and spirits lovers.